ONE VOICE

ONE VOICE

HOUSE AND HERE LIES HENRY

DANIEL MacIVOR

PLAYWRIGHTS CANADA PRESS
TORONTO

PLAYWRIGHTS CANADA PRESS
The Canadian Drama Publisher
215 Spadina Ave., Suite 230, Toronto, ON Canada M5T 2C7
phone 416.703.0013   fax 416.408.3402
orders@playwrightscanada.com • www.playwrightscanada.com

For professional or amateur production rights, please contact
Thomas Pearson at ICM Talent, tpearson@icmtalent.com

The publisher acknowledges the support of the Canadian taxpayers through the
Government of Canada Book Publishing Industry Development Program, the
Canada Council for the Arts, the Ontario Arts Council, and the Ontario Media
Development Corporation.

Canada Council   Conseil des Arts   **ONTARIO ARTS COUNCIL**
for the Arts   du Canada   **CONSEIL DES ARTS DE L'ONTARIO**

Canadä   Ontario

Cover design by Kyra Prew
Cover photo by Guntar Kravis
Type design by Blake Sproule

LIBRARY AND ARCHIVES CANADA CATALOGUING IN PUBLICATION
MacIvor, Daniel, 1962-
One voice / Daniel MacIvor. -- 1st ed.

Plays.
Contents: House -- Here lies Henry.
ISBN 978-0-88754-803-1

I. Title.

PS8575.I86O53 2009   C812'.54   C2009-905614-3

First edition: February 2010
Printed and bound in Canada by Gauvin Press, Gatineau

FOR BUSTER

INTRODUCTION

DANIEL BROOKS

Everything is biographical. What we make, why it is made, how we draw a dog, who it is we are drawn to, why we cannot forget. Everything is collage, even genetics. There is the hidden presence of others in us, even those we have known briefly. We contain them for the rest of our lives, at every border that we cross.

—Michael Ondaatje, *Divisadero*

Who wrote *House*? The simple answer is that Daniel MacIvor wrote the play, with guidance from me. The more complicated answer is *House* was built by many different people, many selves, and was born through many different moments.

In the 1980s, I ran a small theatre company with Don McKellar and Tracy Wright called the Augusta Company. The first show we created together was *Indulgence*. We wanted to indulge ourselves theatrically, we wanted to indulge our mischievous natures. We had seen a play at the Tarragon Theatre that had a very familiar structure, a structure first established in David French's *Leaving Home*. There were an increasing number of Canadian plays with a similar story and structure: a young, sensitive man leaves his Maritime home (he is often a writer), and years later returns for the funeral of his father. The father was a drunk, and the brother left behind by the protagonist is also a drunk; shiftless, unhappy, and a bit thick. The mother is long-suffering. There is a girl who has been waiting for his return, perhaps his first love, and a terrible, hidden secret is, through the action of the play, revealed. We decided to satirize this structure in a play within our play *Indulgence*.

Coincidental with our rehearsal was the production at the Tarragon of Daniel MacIvor's first full-length, multi-character play, which was something like the story I described. The play was not well received, but the writing was original and MacIvor was clearly a great talent. I had never met him. Nonetheless, I intended to call him, to tell him not to be discouraged by the bad reviews, to keep working, that the critics had missed the beauty of the writing. I knew how crucial it was for a young artist to be encouraged by others (I had read that Goethe was ready to give up on *Faust* until Schiller insisted he continue). I never got around to making that call. We continued to work on *Indulgence*, building it around a play within a play called *Sometime Come Often*. The title of Daniel's play had a similar sound: *Somewhere I Have Never Travelled*.

Daniel happened to attend a performance of *Indulgence* with his very good friend from Cape Breton, Caroline Gillis, who had performed in his play. *Somewhere I Have Never Travelled* had closed weeks before. Daniel and Caroline watched our show with their jaws on the floor—having never seen anything like what we were doing and believing we were making fun of their play. They were appalled and enraptured. To this day I maintain that we were not satirizing his play, but another. To this day he does not believe me.

After the show, Daniel and Caroline introduced themselves to Don, Tracy, and I. We had drinks, we all felt each other out, and in a short time we were friends. Daniel suggested he and I go home together, and I graciously declined.

Daniel worked with a loose collection of artists at that time, often at Buddies in Bad Times Theatre. They created a lot of strange and wonderful shows. The group included Ken McDougall, Hillar Lijtoa, Edward Roy, and many other young and vital artists who were experimenting with theatrical form and content. Even though Daniel had been closely collaborating with these people, he approached me with an idea for a one-man show. He had already written a number of very short stories related by theme as well as the beginnings of a character named Victor. He proposed that I direct him in this one-man show called *House*. I agreed, we booked a venue, and soon got down to work.

We began, the two of us in a room, with some ideas. And then we kind of made it up as we went along.

With *House*, the guiding idea for me as a director/dramaturge was that the show would be "an explosion of self." Daniel's body, his voice, his hair and his fingers, his every thought and every memory, his life, all of him, would *be* the show. The show would be a container for all of his selves. We had no idea what form this would take. In fact, we worked for a long time before we discovered the voice—the self—or container for the selves, that was Victor.

This discovery was made at the Theatre Centre in Toronto, several days before our first audience was to appear. We had spent weeks playing with lights, playing with text, and getting nowhere. We knew there was a Victor, but did not know his voice, did not know who he talked to, how he talked, if he sat in a chair or walked the stage aimlessly, whether he spoke from a dark void or in bright, ever-shifting light. There is something that happens in the first weeks of rehearsal, where you live in a world of limitless potential, where you believe chance may deliver something you have never considered. The weeks pass, and suddenly, strangely, you can begin to smell the audience. You know that the kaleidoscope of limitless potential is useless and you have to make some choices. You have to build a house.

We barely had a foundation a week before the audience was to arrive. We had reached an impasse. We had something of a coherent story, but no understanding as to how to tell it. A certain feeling began to creep into our work, a tension, a fear. Daniel was on the stage. I lounged in the audience. At a loss for how to proceed, I asked Daniel, "Why do you want to do this show?" Daniel responded by saying something about connection and truth and contributing something to the world; the kind of thing you would write in a grant proposal. I said, "If you want to be a star, that's all right."

This was an important moment for us. It was the moment in which Daniel's self—the self that wanted to create something special and be acknowledged for doing so, the show-off self—was given encouragement and licence. A certain creative, shameless self was liberated, or perhaps Daniel was liberated from a shameful self. Our work loosened up a bit. Daniel's body came alive and some of the storytelling began to gather a force.

A couple of days later, another event pushed our work forward. We had created about half of the play that exists today, but we did not know how it hung together, and Daniel, as a performer, had no "voice," no centre, no self.

I was sitting in the small auditorium, in the middle of about eighty empty seats. Daniel was on stage. It was less than a week before people would be sitting in those seats, watching Daniel perform. Who would those people be? Some strangers, no doubt, but I don't think Daniel was concerned with the strangers. I suspected that he feared his friends, his "buddies," the people with whom he had been living and working for a number of years. He was afraid that he had betrayed them by working with me, or that they might be jealous and as a result be very harsh and judgmental. In addition, we were young, they were young, and young artists in search of a voice and a self can be very harsh in their judgment of others. As we criticize others, we define ourselves.

I referred to the empty audience, placed each of his absent friends in a specific chair, and said, "There they are. Each of them. What have you got to say to them?"

Immediately he responded, "Are you hating it yet?" The preemptive strike, this anger that came from a deep wound and a bottomless fear became the essence of Victor. Daniel went on, defying his colleagues, addressing each of them personally, challenging them with a sharpness of wit and penetration of insight that was pure joy. He then was able to transform his own fear and anger into the voice of Victor. The voice of Victor had been unleashed.

Soon, he turned that anger on me. We were working on a section in which Victor had been humiliated and was angry. Victor says, "So, in order to calm myself, I counted to thirty on my fingers." I suggested Daniel actually count to thirty, then continue. We ran the section and he counted to thirty silently on his fingers. When he had finished, I told him it took too long, "Maybe you could try twenty." We ran the section again and when Daniel arrived at the moment in question, he said "...so, in order to calm myself, I counted to twenty on my fingers—it used to be counting to thirty but it took too GODDAMNED LONG!" Victor's anger had been unleashed and the verbal inventions came rapidly.

Not only was the text coming alive, but so was Daniel's body. However, he lacked confidence, he lacked a certain physical hook. That finally came when Daniel appeared on stage for one of our final rehearsals with no socks. He lifted his pants and said to me, "I'm not wearing any socks. And I'm not going to tell you why." The feel of his bare feet in loafers grounded him, took him away from his civilian self, helped somehow to confirm the essence of Victor.

We worked long, hard hours for many months on *House*, trying to get every moment on stage "right." We presented it at the Theatre Centre that first time in 1989 and worked on it in different venues for over a year. There is a line in *Here Lies Henry* when, after fumbling a joke or two and playing with his zipper, Henry confesses, "I'm not prepared." Of course, he was prepared. The months of work on *House* were all in preparation for the moment on stage. Daniel's preparation permits absolute spontaneity. Two selves appear on stage: one prepared and in charge of every moment, and one unencumbered, spontaneous, free to do or say anything at all in any way he chooses. It is the first self, the one who has prepared through long hours of work, that creates the possibility of the second, spontaneous self. Preparation is not the mortal enemy of spontaneity, it is the mother of spontaneity.

Daniel performed *House* many times before the play was first published. Just after it was published, he performed it again. He used the published play to go over his lines, but as he carried this book onto the stage, he tossed it aside. There was something strange and dangerous about this inert book, this unchanging written text, this object that existed outside of the subjective self of the performer. We thought of our show as exuberantly alive, unfixed, subject to the inspiration of the moment. The material came out of our lives, our thoughts, our preoccupations, our relationship to one another, but exists as performance in relationship to the other selves in the audience. Our work does not gain focus until we engage with an audience.

The work of creating a play, or anything, is a serious mystery. There is a self, or many selves, that do the work and there is a different self that talks to its friends about the work, or complains about the arduousness of the work. There is a self that works and creates and a self that talks about work and creation, and they are very different from one another.

What Daniel and I did, and still do, is to experiment with notions of the self; our laboratory is the theatre and the object of our experiment is Daniel. However, we also play with one another, from one Daniel to another Daniel, defining the boundary between us, and sometimes erasing it. The plays were originally created by the two of us, two selves experimenting, playing, merging and separating, and eventually Daniel MacIvor would emerge onto the stage, a different self, and play selfishly and selflessly with other people, the audience. These plays are now something else, as are the selves that first created them.

—Daniel Brooks, 2009

HOUSE

House was first workshopped as part of the Research & Development Program at Toronto's Theatre Centre. The play subsequently premiered at the Factory Theatre Studio Café in Toronto in May 1992, produced by da da kamera in association with Factory Theatre.

Performer and writer: Daniel MacIvor
Director and dramaturge: Daniel Brooks
Stage manager: Anne Driscoll
Sound: Greg Rhodes
Set construction: Alex Fallis

House was first mounted in the Mainspace of Theatre Passe Muraille in Toronto in April 1992.

Performer and writer: Daniel MacIvor
Director and dramaturge: Daniel Brooks
Stage manager: Anne Driscoll
Sound: Giovinazzo / Pipco

This is a revised version of the original script, rewritten for the 2007 Toronto remount produced by Buddies In Bad Times Theatre and da da kamera.

A chair centre stage.
Off left a small clamp lamp.
Spotlight on chair.

House lights to black.
We hear the sound of applause, yelping, hooting, bravos.

VICTOR enters.
He sits in the chair. Stands. Regards the chair. Walks front with the chair. Throws it off the stage. Exits.

VICTOR re-enters with another identical chair. Sets it down. Sits on it. Stands. Regards the chair. Walks front with the chair. Throws it off the stage. Exits.

VICTOR re-enters with another identical chair. Sets it down. Sits on it. Relaxes.

With a gesture he cuts the sound of the applause. He snaps his fingers and the stage lights come up full.

VICTOR looks angry and rolls a tiny invisible ball between his thumb and forefinger. He stops.

VICTOR
Hello. Thank you for coming. Thank you for not going some-place else. Thank you for not staying home and watching a show about an angry doctor on teevee. Thank you for coming here.

VICTOR looks angry and rolls a tiny invisible ball between his thumb and forefinger. He stops.

I hate it when they don't do that. Might as well say hello. We're just a room full of people so, hello.

VICTOR looks angry and rolls a tiny invisible ball between his thumb and forefinger. He stops.

I made that up. I did. For group. GROUP! My group: a bunch of fucked-up people sitting around in little wooden chairs in the basement of Our Lady of Perpetual Hypocrisy Church being all fucked-up sitting in a circle jonesing for a cigarette drinking coffee and at the apex of the circle—and I know a cir-cle doesn't have an apex okay but this is not a perfect circle so it has an apex—and at the apex of our circle is our leader: Mister "Call-Me-Joe" (and I won't: call him Joe). You can tell he's our leader because he's the only one in natural fibres, and you gotta respect him for that. Unfortunately his brain isn't present, his brain went missing in 1997, went on a trip with Lucy in the Lollapalooza never came back. And all us fucked-up people sit-ting around him jonesing for a cigarette drinking coffee and being all fucked-up. That's Trish: pills; Harvey: booze; Joyce:

booze; Mrs. Davidson: stuck her head in an oven; be Jennifer: codependency thing with her boyfriend won't go out without him; be Jennifer's boyfriend: nothing wrong with him he's just with Jennifer; be Stew: weird; that girl with the glasses who chews on her split ends and hasn't said anything in three weeks 'cept there's nothing wrong with her but there is TRUST ME! And then there be me. And what's my problem? GUESS!

VICTOR looks angry and rolls a tiny invisible ball between his thumb and forefinger. He stops.

They got Creative Therapy in group. The idea of that is you make things with your hands and your brain is busy keeping your hands busy so your brain doesn't have time to EXPLODE! Making things, useful things like ceramic bears to put cookies in or those little Canadian maple leafs made outta burnt-out matchsticks or candles rolled in sand or macramé— MACRAMÉ! The last bastion of macramé is group—macramé owls with big button eyes you hang on your wall… OR lampshades made outta Popsicle sticks—you know how many Popsicle sticks it takes to make a lampshade? THOUSANDS! Poor Mrs. Davidson wanted one of those Popsicle-stick lampshades so bad she had to get her stomach pumped. She ate all those Popsicles all by herself in the bathtub—and only grape! Why? She came out of that bathtub looking like a big birthmark. She had to go to the hospital to get her stomach pumped, she was big as a 7-Eleven; she was big as a house.

VICTOR stands and thrusts his arms up in victory.

HOUSE!

Lampshade came out looking not too bad if you like that sort of thing—BUT I DON'T! So this one week Mister "Call-Me-Joe" (and I won't: call him Joe) he says to us:

"Hey guys…"

"Guys" or:

"Hey gang…"

Gang or guys he's always calling us. Makes you feel like you should be on a field trip to a museum or something holding on to a rope.

"Hey gang, next week for Creative Therapy I want you to create something at home and then bring it in and show it to the group."

Okay. So I do. I go home, make it up, come in, sit down, do it.

VICTOR looks angry and rolls a tiny invisible ball between his thumb and forefinger. He stops.

Mister "Call-Me-Joe" (and I won't: call him Joe) says:

"Hey Victor man, what wuz that you were doing?"

I say, "Being angry and alone and rolling a tiny invisible ball between my fingers, whaddya think ya jerk!"

Then he says:

"What's inside the ball?"

What's inside the ball? What's inside the invisible ball?

"What's *inside* the ball?"

I say, it's invisible ya moron if there was something in it, it would be visible.

"It's all about the *ball*, Victor."

No, it's not about the *ball*.

"Then what *is* it about?"

It's about me being angry and alone.

And he says:
"That's not *creative*."
Why not?
Yes it is so creative. I should know. I CREATED IT!

Pause. VICTOR walks to the front and lifts his pant legs.

I'm not wearing any socks. And I'm not going to tell you why I'm not wearing any socks because that is part of the mystery of me.

VICTOR returns to his seat. He looks angry and rolls a tiny invisible ball between his thumb and forefinger. He stops.

My buddy Stew from group, he thought it was creative. He said it gave him a feeling—and that's what's creative! It gave him a feeling! If it gives you a feeling it's creative. You don't have to be able to hang it on your wall for it to be creative, you don't have to use glue for it to be creative, if it gives you a feeling it's creative, and my buddy Stew said it gave him a feeling. He said it gave him a feeling of when you're trying to get to sleep at night and there's a big ball of rubber on the ceiling and a spoon taking scoops out of it and whipping them at you, he says it's a feeling you get in your teeth.

Stew's weird.

Now you might think that I'm weird but I'm not. I'm fucked-up. There's a fundamental difference between weird and fucked-up. You are born weird, you get fucked-up. You can't be born fucked-up or get weird. You have to be born weird. I'm fucked-up. Stew is WEIRD!

You want first-hand evidence of that you invite him to your

place. You invite him to your place, he will steal, even if you're his friend he will steal from you and not smart things either, stupid things, won't steal the teevee or the toaster or the bowl of change by the door, he'll steal stupid things like steal the handles off your kitchen cupboards so you come home three o'clock in the morning want something to eat don't want to turn the light on... *(reaches for non-existent handle)* steal the thing out of the back of the toilet that floats, he'll steal the round things you got on the bottom of the chairs in the living room so they don't dent the carpet, steal the charger off your cellphone! You leave him alone in a room with a cellphone on a charger he'll take the charger off the cellphone put it in his pocket when he goes it's gone and what good's a cellphone without a charger and what good's it to him—can't sell it—what good's a charger without a cellphone. Unless of course Stew's been to your place! OR! Is he weird? This one week after group we're going for coffee Stew wants to stop off and get some gum 'cause he's off the butts...

Don't mind if I do.

> *VICTOR looks on his person for cigarettes. He can't find any. He forgets what he was saying. He tries to rally.*

Butts...
Coffee...
Group...
Stew...
Gum.
GUM!
We're going for gum. We're going for coffee after group Stew wants some gum so I say, Hey let's go in this variety store

because variety is the spice of life—but no, Stew has to go in the supermarket. Why? Because he's fixated on supermarkets. Why? Because he likes the lighting, AND because he likes the dairy section because you can stick your head in a fridge and pretend to be looking for something. That's the other thing about weird people, they're always complaining they have hot heads because their brains are overworked from thinking about shapes and colours all the time. "Shapes and colours, shapes and colours, the whole world's made up of shapes and colours." IGNORANCE IS BLISS!

So I'm there in the gum section: "What kind a gum you want Stew? Stew? Stew?"

But Stew's not there, no, he's in the dairy section, I gotta drag him out of the dairy section. So we get the gum we're standing at the cash to pay there's this woman in front of us with a whole cartload of processed food with which she is going to go home and kill her family: Ding Dongs, Ring Dings, Cheez Product, Meat Roll, Bleach, Discount Cola. She's got multiples of everything that's bad for you. Full cart full. Now, she turns around, sees Stew with gum with me with nothing, she doesn't say anything. Does Stew say anything? NO!

Doesn't say:

"Excuse me, lady, I only got a pack of gum you got a whole cartload of stuff mind if I go ahead of you?"

NO! He just stands there while she takes out each and every package of poison puts it on the counter punches it into her calculator each and every package of poison puts it on the counter punches it into her calculator. I'm getting TENSE! So I take a trip, which is something I do when I get tense. I look around for something to take a trip on and I take a trip. I see the bird on the box of Froot Loops in her cart—she's got THREE boxes of

Froot Loops! So I'm on my trip: I'm sitting on the counter in her kitchen, I'm invisible, her two sets of identical triplet boys are sitting at the table, all six years old, she's on the phone, talking to her sister in Medicine Hat, the boys are starving, she throws a box of Froot Loops on the table, they rip it open, eating the Froot Loops dry, getting little pieces of cardboard caught in their throats and making those little coughs, she hangs up the phone throws the boys in the basement locks the door, no wonder they got such bad eyes they're locked in the basement all day, no wonder their teeth are rotted out of their heads they're eating dry Froot Loops!

Okay. So I'm back in the supermarket. And not a dent made in the cart! Why? While I was in her kitchen she ran off to aisle seven got another dozen packages of Ding Dongs. I'm getting TENSE! So I do my calming action which I got from group which is counting to thirty very slowly on my fingers and thinking of waves, used to be counting to fifty but took TOO GODDAMN LONG! I get to twelve it's a tidal wave so I turn to the woman give her one of these: *(raps himself on the side of the head three times with his knuckles) one* of these: *(again)* on the side of the head.

"Hey is anybody home, is anybody home at all? That's the problem with this country there's nobody HOME!"

Well you woulda thought I shot her. Cops there everything, and they're charging me with assault. Assault? With what? With this? *(two raps)* What's that? *(two raps)* That's a symbol. *(two raps)* That's a metaphor. They're charging me with assault with a metaphor.... "Stew, back me up, Stew, back me up, Stew, back me up." No. Why? Stew's gone! They're charging me with assault with a metaphor meanwhile the real criminal is fifteen blocks away with a mouth full of STOLEN Bubblicious!

That's the world we live in welcome to it.
Couple of days later I catch up to Stew:
"You idiot!"
He says to me:
"Man you're weird."
ME! And I gotta remind him one more time:
"Stew, my friend, Stew, you are weird, me I'm just FUCKED-UP!"

VICTOR steps forward. He picks up the clamp lamp, he makes a gesture and the lights go to black. VICTOR turns on the clamp lamp and illuminates his face with it.

A man goes to a fortune teller. The fortune teller tells the man: "You mus buy a hoose and move into dee hoose unt stay dere for vun yeer and den dis yeer vill bring for you great sadness unt great joy."
Well the man was very excited when he heard about this because up to that point his life had been plain and unremarkable. And so the man finds a house, he buys the house, he moves into it and stays there for one year. And any time the phone would ring, and any time there was a knock on the door, and any time a car would pull into the driveway, the man would prepare himself for great sadness or great joy. And even though whenever the phone would ring it was only ever a wrong number, and even though whenever there was a knock on the door it was only ever two guys in ties trying to save his soul, and even though whenever a car would pull into the driveway it was only ever to turn around and go the other way, the man would always remember 1997 as his best year.

VICTOR turns off the clamp lamp. Black.
Lights up.
VICTOR circles the chair suspiciously.

(calling offstage) Mary Ann!
(tearfully) Mary Ann.

Mary Ann used to be my third cousin then we got married now she's my wife. Ma introduced us. She had us both for dinner then she took me in the kitchen and told me: Marry your cousin. I thought she was nuts but later we're sitting around the tube watching the Shroud of Turin on *Man Alive* and I look over at Mary Ann and the blue light of the Shroud of Turin on *Man Alive* is dancing on her face and she looks over at me and goes: *(mouthing)* "Boring." "Boring." So I fall in love with her. MISTAKE! So we get married. MISTAKE! Why? Because I neglect to find out before we get married that the woman can't stand me. And why can't she stand me? You got two days? But the main reason why she can't stand me is because of my job and it's not my fault it's my job it's just my job it's not my fault.

I was gonna be an engineer. But I'm not.

I was gonna be an engineer.

I was gonna be an engineer for two reasons. First reason why I was going to be an engineer was because engineers are the guys who figure out how to build things so they don't fall down. Figure out how to build the floor so the ceiling won't cave in, figure out how to build the ceiling so the walls won't bend. Now that's useful information, especially if you've ever had anything fall on you.

The second reason why I wanted to be an engineer was because THEY'RE SO FUNNY! Oh yeah, engineers are the guys who, on April Fool's, put a Volkswagen on the roof of the cafeteria or fill the dean's office with liquid insulation. NOW THAT'S FUNNY! But it is to be *respected* because it's not a joke. It's not. Any idiot can tell a joke, I could tell a joke, but it's not a joke, it's a... prank! Ah! And a prank is to be *respected* because it involves *camaraderie*! Ah! Camaraderie! I never had any camaraderie. Camaraderie was something I saw twenty-five yards away in a field with a bunch of guys and a ball. I never had any camaraderie—if we had violins we'd play them—you know, camaraderie, when you're a kid and you're gonna put a frog in a paper bag and set it on fire and throw it on somebody's doorstep, you gotta figure out whose doorstep, who's gonna catch the frog, who's not scared of frogs, who's gonna put the frog in the bag, who's gonna set the bag on fire, who's not scared of getting burnt. You know, camaraderie. And engineers are the most camaraderistic people in the whole world and I always imagined that when they'd be doing their prank, they'd all be up in some office where they broke in late at night with a skeleton key and they'd be putting the photocopier in the water cooler and then when they were finished they'd come down into the street being all quiet and happy and proud of their prank and the sun would just be coming up and they'd be saying beautiful poetic things to one another like:

"See ya tomorrow."

"Call ya Friday."

"Wanna go for breakfast?"

And that might not sound like poetry to you but it does if you never heard it and I never did.

I was gonna be an engineer but I'm not.

I clean septic tanks.

Of course I don't actually clean them myself. I work in the office. Millard's Sanitary Vacuum Service Office Worker.

Speaking of fashion: I prefer a slip-on shoe, we've discussed the socks, a polyester slack, an open-neck shirt, a sporty sports jacket, they say clothes make the man I wish they'd make the bed, I wish they'd make the money.

VICTOR is lost. He tries to find his way back.

Money.
Mommy.
Mother.
Father.
Father!
My father was in the septic-tank business. He installed 'em. And he was a bit of a septic-tank hero because he saved a kid from downing in a septic tank one time and so he had his picture in the paper and became a hero so that whenever you thought of septic tanks you thought of my father and whenever you thought of my father you thought of septic tanks. That happens with heroes. That's association. Like you think of war you think of soldier you think of cop you think of donut. Like that. And when my father left my mother to go and join the circus... and that's another story, too long no time can't tell it... she went into this deep depression and said the only way she would get out of it is if I went into the septic-tank business or became a priest and I said to her:

"Ma, how can I become a priest I'm not a FAG!"

And I can say that because I was a fag in my last life, and I'm gonna be a fag in my next life, or hey I don't know... talk to me after the show.

But it's not a show.... It's my life. It's my... *(stands and thrusts his arms up in victory)* HOUSE!

But you know what really burns me up? That was twenty-three years ago; I go into the septic-tank business, my mother's still depressed. Why? Because she won't live her own life she insists on living her life through me and if you were living your life through me wouldn't you be depressed! But I say to her, Ma, get your own life, would you please get your own life! But she can't because then she would have to go out into the world and talk to people and admit that she's a human being and she won't admit that she's a human being. Why? Because human beings are what? BAD! And they stink, well they must they sell enough deodorant. But us huh, we're not afraid to admit that we're bad and we stink are we!

Are we!

Are we?

VICTOR snaps his fingers. The stage goes black. He sniffs in the darkness. He turns on the clamp lamp illuminating his face.

There was a man who had a house and every Thursday night he would invite all of his friends over, feed them dinner, and then get drunk. And when he got drunk he would tell each and every one of his friends in a very loud voice in a very direct way what was their problem. And then he would get drunker and tell each and every one of his friends in a very loud voice in a very direct way exactly what it was about them that made them one in a million. And every Thursday night the house was packed because, well, to hear that you are one in a million, how sweet it is to hear such words of love. And every Thursday night the house was packed because everybody knew that when the man told them what their problem was he was just drunk.

VICTOR turns off the clamp lamp.
Black. He snaps his fingers. Lights up.
VICTOR takes a piece of green indoor/outdoor carpeting
from his pocket.

Does that look like grass to you?

He discards it.

I've been with the company for twelve years. Twelve years at Millard's Sanitary Vacuum Service. That's three years for every desk in the office. That's six months for every fabric partition between the desks. That's one day for every day I had to hear Tom the guy at the next desk say, "Well somebody's got to do the dirty work ha ha ha."

The immediate reality of my reality of my... space would be me and my desk, the frosted-glass office of the King of Millard's Sanitary Vacuum Service, Mister Millard, be Brenda his personal and private secretary who is such a Luddite she's still got the office on dial-up, be Tom the guy with the sense of humour like a head cold, then there be the big desk by the window, that be Andrew.

Andrew.

"Hey sport..."

Sport.

"Hey sport, too bad you don't got a view..."

He's got the view. He's got the view of the parking lot and St. Jude's School for Pubescent Girls across the street.

"...too bad you don't got a view, there's a little filly, there's a little filly right now, wouldn't mind taking that little filly for a little t-t-trot around the t-t-track."

Andrew's an idiot.

He went to university for two years he's got this tattoo of an expression on his face "I been to university for two years" who cares! He's always saying stuff like: "If you knew anything about b-b-body language you wouldn't be sitting like that right now."

He's an idiot.

But Millard loves him. Oh yeah. He loves him. Andrew's been there eighteen months. Eighteen months! What's that? That's not even a human being, you can't even form a complete sentence at eighteen months. But Millard says to him: "Call me Jim." Call him Jim?!

I been there twelve years he never told me to call him Jim. He had Andrew out to his place to parties there. Mrs. Millard and Doris, Andrew's wife, joined a club together. Millard doesn't even know I'm married. Then Andrew goes on vacation two weeks comes back, first day back, comes into the office standing right in front of my desk Millard comes out of his office over to Andrew RIGHT IN FRONT OF MY DESK gives him... a hug... a *hug*. He *hugs* him. Why didn't he just pour hot wax in my ears? So I get depressed and when I get depressed I get angry and when I get angry I get depressed so to break the cycle I do something I haven't done in ten years I go looking for the old man. He's easy enough to find because he's still with the circus, he's got a little act worked up: Saddest Man in the World. So I find the circus I go to the gate tell the guy who I'm looking for he sends me down to the tent by the weight-guessing. Get there big sign on the tent: "SEE HERE SADDEST MAN IN THE WORLD" a line going in one side people all pink and dizzy from the Tilt-a-Whirl coming out the other side all grey and saaaaad. So I pay my money, five bucks, and get in line and so how it works is there's this wall with a hole in it and you stick your head in the hole and this is what you see: you see him and you think: What, he doesn't even look sad! He looks bored, this is a rip. I want my money back. Five bucks! I want my money back. But then before you can look away his face goes all foggy and it's not him anymore, it changes into an actual real flesh of you, but you when you were your saddest, saddest ever in your whole life and you look and you think Oh My God I Can't Even Look At That so you look down at your feet but your feet aren't there 'cause your head's in a hole! So you look back and that's when it hits you... right there, in that secret of the secret, that place that you know that you know but you're afraid to say you knew you knew that place deep down deep deep deep deeper than your stomach deeper than your dreams deep down to that place that's just this big and it's round and wet on the inside that's that thing of "Human beings aren't built to last," that's that thing of all it takes for you to never ever be or ever have been or ever be again all it takes is: *(He holds up a tiny invisible ball between his thumb and forefinger, then suddenly brings his thumb and forefinger together, squashing the ball, making a tiny fart-like sound with his lips.)* ...That's worth five bucks.

VICTOR plays "Amazing Grace" by putting his head back, plugging his nose, and banging on his throat with the side of his hand creating the sound of bagpipes. After a few lines he stops and weeps. He continues. Midway through, he stops.

Ah you know how it ends.

He approaches the edge of the stage conspiratorially.

I know it's a theatre.
I do.
I know it's a theatre. I know it's a stage. I know it's a chair. I
know it's a light.

*He snaps his fingers. A bank of coloured lights comes on
behind him.*

I know it's a light.

He snaps his fingers. The bank of lights goes out.

I know you're a house.

*VICTOR snaps his fingers. The house lights come up. He
smilingly starts down off the stage.*

Oh oh. Oh oh. Oh no. Here he comes! He's ruining everything! I didn't know it was THAT KIND of PLAY! Stop! Stop!
Now you wish you stayed home and watched that angry doctor
on teevee, huh? Teevee doesn't get up and walk around behind
you, don't have to turn your head to watch teevee, never get a
sore neck from teevee.
Nice theatre, huh?
Other than the leaky roof and the crappy seats and the rats in
the basement and the sirens every ten seconds it's a very high-
society type establishment.

*VICTOR gets himself a glass of water—perhaps there is a bar
set up at the back of the room—perhaps he has to step out
into the lobby. All the while he continues talking.*

And plus if you run out of crack you only have to walk a few feet past the front door to score. GOTTA LOVE THAT! I saw a play here once. It was pretty damn good other than for the fact that it SUCKED! I wanted to do the whole show here in front of these doors but they wouldn't let me. Why? Fire regulations. Okay then how about a little campfire on stage—you know storytelling and all that. No. Why? Fire regulations. They're crazy for fire regulations here. They're dying to have a fire to see if all the regulations work.

VICTOR returns to the stage.

"Oh thank God he's back up there. What was the point of all that?"

VICTOR pours the glass of water over his head.

Okay here's something.

VICTOR weeps theatrically.

Acting!
They give awards for acting. Why? Best liar. Thank you very much. Best-written lie. Thank you very much. Best-directed lie. Thank you very much.
I know all about awards because I won one once.

VICTOR snaps his fingers. The house lights go out.
He loses his place.

I did. I won...

One.
Two.
Four.
Eight.
Late.
Work.
Sell.
SELL!
Salesperson of the Month. I won Sanitary Vacuum
Salesperson of the Month and I don't remember what month
it was but it was at least twenty-eight or as many as thirty-
one days and either way you look at it that's a lot of days to
be the best. And I was. And it wasn't in-office either. It was
the Greater Metropolitan Salesperson Umbrella Organization
for the greater metropolitan region. And that takes in sales of
every kind. I didn't even know the organization existed until I
got the letter but hey I wasn't going to argue. Sanitary Vacuum
Salesperson of the Month. As soon as I got the letter I get it all
worked out in my head how it's gonna be night of. Night of me
and Mary Ann take a cab down to the Ramada Inn where the
awards are being held. (Take a cab because I'm on the booze
then. Don't drink and drive.) Get there walk into the Ramada
go to reception "Excuse me where are the awards being held?"
she goes "Oooo" points us off to the meeting room walk in the
place is filled with people sitting at these long tables with white
paper tablecloths drinking tomato juice all looking at us thinking: "That guy looks like a winner," and "Isn't she lovely." I'm
pleased, she's beaming. Sit at the head table have our hot turkey
dinner and as many rye and gingers AS I WANT they call my
name I get up receive my plaque with my name and my picture
on it make a speech about my father the septic-tank hero the

23

crowd is warmed by my reminiscences, some people are crying, everybody claps, I with my wife on one arm my award
under the other leave, walk out of the Ramada Inn and begin
my new and happy life.

And if you believe that you haven't been paying attention up
to now.

Turns out night of is Mary Ann's Girls' Night Out ("Lingerie
party, sorry can't make it.") Fine, I go by myself. Take a cab
down, driver takes me the long way around, fine everybody's
gotta make a living. Get there nobody knows anything about
any awards spend twenty minutes looking for the room finally
find it level two basement. Fine. Walk in there's about a dozen
people sitting around watching teevee on their cellphones.
Fine. Turns out dinner is hot turkey *sandwiches*. Fine. Turns
out... it's a *cash* bar. Fine. Turns out the whole thing is put
on by the Amway people and they do a big demonstration of
Amway and explain how we should get out of whatever business we're in and get into Amway. Fine. I get my plaque it's got
my name spelled wrong and a picture of ANDREW on it. Fine.
Turns out that I don't get to make a speech because everybody
there's getting a salesperson of the month award. Fine. After
we all go out to this strip club and watch some skinny blond
woman take her bra off on a plaid blanket and throw up. Fine. I
get home Mary Ann's sitting in front of the tube I say:

"Oh Mary Ann..."

She says:

"I'm watching this."

It's a show about ALGAE! FINE! So I sit down I ask myself a
question. I ask myself: What's Wrong With Me.

Yeah yeah I know you all got an answer to that but I'm not
asking you I'm asking me and that is an important point in a

person's life when you can ask yourself a personal question like that and I'm asking myself: What's Wrong With Me?

So I get a dictionary I look up "me."

Me: objective case of I.

Okay, look up "I."

I: subjective case of me.

Objective case of I. Subjective case of me. Objective case of I. Subjective case of me. Objective case…. Subjective case… AND I REALZE! The problem's not with ME! The problem's not with I! The problem's with… the case! THE CASE! YES! CELEBRATORY MUSIC PLEASE!

Loud rock music. VICTOR dances in short, sharp movements then suddenly, after about fifteen seconds, makes a gesture to cut the music. Silence.

So I am going to change my life.

And I'm not going to join the Y. Why? That's what everybody does when they want to change their life, join the Y. Why? What? So that I can build my body up so strong I'll never get out of it. No thank you. And I'm not going to leave my wife. That's what everybody else does when they want to change their life. I am not going to leave Mary Ann because I tried that before and it was a nightmare in Technicolor. This one time I leave Mary Ann because we're getting all these invoices from *Swingles Magazine* made out to "Veronica, Mistress of Discipline," I don't even want to know, I leave. I pack up a suitcase I go to Stew's place, knock on the door. Stew's girlfriend Darlene opens it takes one look at me with a suitcase: "Noooo way!" SLAM! That's fine, it's her prerogative to not stand me because she thinks I'm a fucked-up influence on Stew because she knows how weird he is and you gotta respect her for that. Also that Christmas party two years ago and we WERE SO both drunk Darlene… but that's another story too long no time can't tell it, so I leave I go to my sister's place. Lucky for me my sister can stand me. She's got a little bit of a problem though, she's got this thing with annulments. She's had five annulments. It's easy for her to get them because she used to go out with this bisexual guy Dave who was a priest and now he's a bishop so she just calls him up:

"Oh Dave, it's just not working out with this guy…"

So Dave just does a *(bangs himself on the forehead with his fist)* annulled. *(bangs himself on the forehead with his fist)* Didn't happen. *(bangs himself on the forehead with his fist)* Annulled. *(bangs himself on the forehead with his fist)* Didn't happen. *(bangs himself on the forehead with his fist)* Didn't happen. Now that's a stroke of brilliance huh? The Catholic church, they're something else. What nine-year marriage? What six kids? Didn't happen! So anyway my sister's just getting her fifth annulment, which is good for me because she has space for me to stay at her place BUT…. She's got this dog. Now that doesn't sound strange that a person would have a dog but if you knew my sister, she was all her life terrified of dogs. She used to have this recurring nightmare when she was a kid about all these dogs in pantsuits… too long no time… but she would wake up screaming "MY BONES! MY BONES!" But now she's got this dog, and this dog is not a normal dog, this dog is huge… Hugo she calls him… and Hugo is huge, this dog is big as a Lexus, this dog is big as a house.

VICTOR stands and thrusts his arms up in victory.

HOUSE!

And my sister is big as a bug, big as a minute. So I think this is strange so next day I got group, I go in they're all playing Word of the Week and I hate Word of the Week so it comes to me for my turn I say.... Hey... and I tell them about my sister and Hugo the dog, and Mister "Call-Me-Joe" (and I won't: call him Joe) he says:

"Hey Victor, man, I think it's obvious what your problem is."

Oh yeah hotshot what's my problem?

And that girl with the glasses who hasn't said anything in three weeks takes her split ends out of her mouth and she says:

"You're jealous of the dog."

Great.

I'm jealous of a dog.

GREAT ANOTHER PILE OF SHIT TO CARRY AROUND WITH ME FOR THE REST OF MY LIFE I'M JEALOUS OF A DOG!

But no I'm not. I'm not jealous of a dog because there is no dog, I annul it. I go back to my sister's place with her and no dog. Easy.

THEN this one night I'm home early, I'm supposed to home late I'm not I'm home early walk up the stairs to the apartment all this racket coming from inside I walk in the place is filled with dogs. All these drunk dogs in the kitchen rooting through the cupboards and the drawers, all these dogs lined up for the can, I go in the living room they got a red light bulb in the lamp and all these dogs in couples all over the place, this Luther Vandross music is playing and in the corner is my sister slow dancing with Hugo the dog! NO THANK YOU! I'm on my way out I almost get killed trying to break up these two Irish setters fighting over the last of the pâté and I'm trying to explain to them that there's a half-dozen cans of pâté in the cupboard but that doesn't matter they can't open the cans they got no THUMBS! So I leave this nightmare… and I go to my mother's place, which may be a stupid move but hey this is serious, I'm thinking about a divorce, this is serious stuff here I gotta talk to somebody about it. So I go to my mother's sit down she's sitting in front of the tube as per usual. The teevee's always on there, it's like a dialysis machine, you even look at the remote she goes into a seizure, but I gotta talk to somebody! So:

"Ma.

Ma.

Ma?

Ma?

Ma!

Ma!

MAAAAAAA!"

Nothing.

Okay then:

"Ma, I'm thinking about getting a divorce from Mary Ann."

ZING! She's on me, she says:

"If you get a divorce from your wife you will spend an eternity in hell."

Oh yeah?

I say to her:

"Oh yeah Ma, well that's okay, I already got my ticket, it's one-way and I'm taking YOU WITH ME!"

Well. Then there's this explosion. I'm out for…. Well you don't know how long you're out when you're out 'cause you're out but I'm out for say three hours. I come to, the room is filled with smoke and the smell of sulphur. Smoke clears a bit I look up on the ceiling… MA! There's my mother on the ceiling. Her head is turned right around on her body, her eyes are big as turnips, her tongue is hanging out of her mouth about three feet all pointy on the end lashing around the room slitting the curtains... MA...! catches me here on the arm, sixteen stitches, she's got all this Latin coming out of her mouth, steam coming out of her ears and her perm is curling and uncurling, curling and uncurling, curling and uncurling.... MA PLEASE! I'm trying to get her down. MA PLEASE! I'm there a week and a half trying to get her down off the ceiling and it's getting uglier because the place is filled with goats and I'm allergic so finally I relent... "Okay Ma, I'll go back to Mary Ann."

Zip. She's back in the La-Z-Boy, Paid Promotional Programming on the tube, nothing happened.

So I am not going to leave Mary Ann.

And I am not going to join the Y. Why?

But I know what I'm going to do.

I know what I'm going to do.

This is the part about the house.

In the lunchroom.

Sitting at my table.

Meatloaf sandwich. White bread. Processed cheese. Everything's pretty much as per normal. Tom's telling Helen Keller jokes to the coffee machine.

Brenda's on the phone seeing if she can get the office back on rotary dial.

Andrew and Millard at their table practically all over one another as per usual. I'm sitting there moving a cup back and forth. Something I like to do to help me think. Move an object back and forth very quickly so it becomes long and blurry. It helps readjust my reality. And I think: Yes. I'm gonna do it. I wait till Andrew goes to the can I get up go over to Millard. Standing there a minute before he notices me. He looks up.

VICTOR snaps his fingers. Light shift: a single red spotlight on him.

"hi sir how you doing goodta seeya listen i saw your car in the parking lot you got a wax job huh looks great i got a wax job on mine last spring fifty bucks but it's work it ah listen i don't wanna take up too much of your time but we got some work done on the place and my wife and i were talking... oh yeah years... Mary Ann... Mary Ann... and you know i been here twelve years... yeah...! and we never sat down had like a dinner and i was thinking that maybe you might be interested in coming out to dinner at my... house..."

And he hems and he haws and he talks about his busy schedule and his nephew's wedding and I say:

"please... sir?"

And he says:

VICTOR snaps his fingers. Light restores to normal stage light.

"Yeah I'll come."

A COUP! So I got two weeks till night of. I get my sister we go down to the bank she co-signs a loan, hundred and twenty thousand dollars. I get a landscaping job on the front yard floodlights on the house, get new carpeting living room, hallway, stairs, get the rec room finally finished, get all new fixtures in the bathroom... and a bidet! Get whole new gut job on the kitchen, ceiling, floor, brand-new appliances... stainless steel! I come down morning of night of the place is like a dream, it's like a place off teevee where the family sits around the fireplace playing board games, it's perfect... except for the kitchen floor. Ran out of money workmen walked out whaddya gonna do. But that's okay, I'm late I gotta leave, but it's okay 'cause Mary Ann can do it! Go in the kitchen Mary Ann's sitting on a box of tiles talking on the phone. Sees me hangs up.

"Who were you talking to Mary Ann?"

"Nobody."

...If I had a dime for every time Mary Ann was on the phone talking to nobody, leaving the house going nowhere or coming home after having done nothing I'd be a TRILLIONAIRE! But that's okay and I'm explaining to Mary Ann about how I'm late I gotta leave but how the tiles are so easy...

"They're easy."

And they are.

"They're self-adhesive."

They're self-adhesive.

"They're black and white."

Black tile white tile black tile white tile black tile white tile easy.

"Hey Mary Ann, you don't even have to know your colours just the difference between black and white ha ha..."

Mary Ann goes for the phone.

"Who ya calling Mary Ann?"

"Nobody."

"MARY ANN I AM DOING ALL THIS FOR YOU!"

She gets up comes over to me standing very close I can smell her hair....

Then I go on this trip.... This is long, long ages ago, haven't thought about this in years, we're at this party, Mary Ann's sitting in this group of people she's telling a story, I'm standing apart from them, can't hear what she's saying but I'm watching, and everybody is really listening to her, and she finishes... and everybody laughs, everybody, and not this made up "please like me" laugh but a real true surprising laugh where you laugh and surprise even yourself and make this ugly sound *(snort)* and I'm looking at Mary Ann smiling and everyone around her doing this real, surprising laughter and I'm thinking Oh My God... she's mine...

So I'm thinking this and standing on the ripped-up kitchen floor Mary Ann standing very close to me, she leans in even closer and she says: "You're full of shit." And that is so cheap! She's always doing that shit metaphor on me because of my job and it's not my fault it's my job it's just my job, I was going to be an engineer I was. But I'm not! But she's always doing that shit metaphor, you're full of shit, you suck shit, you eat shit, it is so cheap. But it pushes my BUTTON! So I leave, I'm late, I leave. Get in the car put on my *The Secret* CD that I got from group. Oh, and what's the secret? Positive thinking. FUCK OFF!!! But it sort of does the trick and re-channels my anger. Get to work everything's pretty much as per normal. Tom's telling light-bulb jokes out the window. Brenda's digging a firepit so she can send the invoices by smoke signal. But then things take a turn for the better: Andrew calls in sick! Then, I'm standing by my desk Millard comes over to me, gives me one of these: *(hits himself in his shoulder with his fist)*. One of these: *(again)*. And that is just as... that's better than a hug *(again)* 'cause you can still feel it later. Throughout the day he gives me several of these *(again)*. Four-thirty comes Millard comes out of his office over to me at my desk says:

"You wanna go for a brew?"

"YES... yeah sure okay."

We go to the pub next door. I just have coffee 'cause I'm off the booze then but he has beer and I'm thinking if anybody walked in now didn't know us they'd look over and say:

"Oh yeah couple of buddies out for a drink after work one guy having coffee one guy having beer buddy must be on the wagon."

They wouldn't even know the truth!

And Millard is really talking to me. He's asking me questions about myself.

He's asking me where I went to school:

"Where'd you go to school?"

He's asking me about my parents:

"Are your parents still living?"

He's asking me what's my favourite ball team:

"What's you favourite—"

And we got the same favourite ball team! And not the local guys either, these other guys from away who nobody else even likes.

He tells me a dirty joke! (Which I won't repeat.)

Seven-thirty we pile into our cars, I get in mine he gets in his. Driving along get to my neighbourhood and I think, Yes I am glad I'm paying these high property taxes because this is a NICE neighbourhood! I look in my rear-view mirror, and behind me is my boss, coming to dinner, at my house.

Now I don't know if I just knew this because sometimes you think back on something and you think, Oh yeah I knew that, or if I knew because the floodlights weren't on the house like I asked that they be.

VICTOR snaps his fingers, stage lights out. In the black:

So it's all dark. I get out of the car. Millard comes up to me: "Wasn't your wife expecting us ha ha?"

I go in the house, Millard right behind me, walk in the kitchen, turn on the light.

VICTOR uses the clamp lamp to illuminate either his face or areas of the room he is describing.

OH YES Mary Ann's got the tiles down. Thank you Mary Ann! But instead of black tile white tile black tile white tile black tile white tile she started with the black tiles and when she ran out of black tiles she started with the white tiles. She's got all the black tiles together and all the white tiles together. FABULOUS!

Noise in the living room. Go in the living room. Millard right behind me. And there's Mary Ann. And this is what she's wearing:

Big black boots up to here... no, higher, here, rubber panties, no bra no shirt no nothing, a leather mask that covers her whole head with a zipper for the mouth and in her hand she's got this long piece of hose and she sort of flicks it at me like: Get Lost! Sitting in the easy chair by the teevee all tied up and wearing a diaper is... ANDREW!

"Hey sport, join the p-p-party!"

Mary Ann looks at Millard gives him one of these:

(calling with his index finger) "C'mere."

I look at Millard he's got this zombie-Christmas-morning look on his face he looks at Mary Ann and says:

"VERONICA!"

She says to Millard:

"Call me Mommy, you bastard."

Like I need this.

I leave.

Get a room in a motel for the night, go into work the next day feeling like a real jerk, Andrew called in "sick" again, Millard's not there didn't in call in doesn't have to owns the place. Two o'clock phone call comes, for me, it's Mary Ann:

"Please make other arrangements for the rest of your life."

Click. Buzzzzz. Two-thirty, phone call comes, for me, it's Millard's lawyer, and he says:

"Mister Millard would be interested in sitting down having a meeting with you to discuss the possibility of purchasing your house."

He wants to buy my house.

He wants to buy my house.

He wants to...

He wants to buy my house.

And I think about this.

VICTOR spins the clamp lamp in wide circles over his head.

And I think about it and I think about it and I think about it and I think about it and I think about it ...

He catches the light and brings it to rest on his face.

And I think about it and I think:

Hey, my boss, with my wife, in my house, hey, that kind a connection, that kind a connection, it's just a matter of time before it's:

VICTOR turns the clamp lamp off and snaps his fingers.

Stage lights up full.

"Hey Jimbo, how ya doin! We won last night, pretty good, huh? Listen, anything you need? Look I'll call ya tomorrow, see ya Friday, wanna go for breakfast? Anything you need? Need a lift? Need some cash? Need a wife? Need a house? The shirt off my back? A pound of flesh perhaps?

VICTOR snaps his fingers. Black. Throughout the following a spot comes up very slowly on VICTOR in the chair.

A man and a woman were destined to meet and fall in love. They were supposed to meet while both were working in the mailroom of a large publishing company but due to an accident of fate this never happened. Instead the man secured a job behind the counter in a bookstore and the woman secured a job in a library. And even though the library was just around the corner from the bookstore and even though the bookstore was just around the corner from the library so severe and serious was this accident of fate that in twenty-five years neither chanced to glance so much at the back of the other's head.

The woman lived in a two-bedroom apartment in a four-storey walk-up with her sister, and the man lived in a four-bedroom house near the plant by the tracks with two guys he knew from his chess club.

For a time both the man and the woman felt that something was missing from their lives but then they decided that this was just the feeling of being human.

Then one day the man decides what he needs in his life is a place of his own. So he calls up a real estate agent and makes plans to see a "lovely little house" by the lake at twelve o'clock on Wednesday afternoon.

And one day the woman decides what she needs in her life is a place of her own. So she calls up a real estate agent and makes plans to see a "lovely little house" by the lake at twelve-thirty on Wednesday afternoon.

And since the man was always late and the woman was always early they both arrive at the same time.

And they stand beside one another, nervous, strangers, until they are introduced by the real estate agent, and as they shake hands and look into one another's eyes, they both become filled with all the experiences they had been destined to have:

Five summers by the ocean, a year in Spain, the fat grey cat, the funny blue car, the antique bookcase, the wooden shutters, the ivy on the porch, the mornings over tea, the fear of heights, the red-wine stain on the white dress, the terrible fight about the girl down the road... on and on and more and more until the man and the woman become so filled with love that they then and there in the "lovely little house" by the lake, they then and there, explode.

Black. In the black:

But as the real estate agent will tell you:
"Oh it was a glorious explosion."

VICTOR snaps his fingers. Stage lights up full.

This is last week. I go to group. They're playing Word of the Week and God I hate Word of the Week.... Gets to me I say, "Hey, my mother is possessed by the devil, my father is the saddest man in the world, my sister is in love with a dog, the one I love does not love me, and I got no place to live."

Mister "Call-Me-Joe" (and I will not: call him Joe) he says:

"Hey Victor man, we're playing Word of the Week, right all right?"

All right, I sit down I shut up I don't say another word all night.

After, everybody's talking about who's going for coffee. I leave. I can hear Mister "Call-Me-Joe" (and I don't have to say it again):

"Hey Vic!"

Uh uh. I leave. And I walk out of that place with the walk of a man who is not coming back.

I'm sitting at Denny's having my sixth cup of coffee playing with my smokes and thinking about going outside to finish off the pack this girl I don't know comes in, sits at my booth. She's got a book, she says, mind if I read out loud? I go: Wha? She thinks that's "yes" she starts reading. But real quiet-like so you can hear she's saying something but you can't hear what she's saying. After a couple of pages she gets bored and stops. She's looking at me, she's looking at my smokes, she looks at me she says: smoking is bad for you. I say: LEAK THAT TO THE MEDIA!

Then we start talking and she tells me about her life and that she's Scottish and then she starts to cry 'cause she does have a pretty bad life so I play the bagpipes on my throat which is something I do and she likes that 'cause she's Scottish right. We talk some more and I tell her about group and about Creative Therapy and I show her my being angry and alone and roll-ing a tiny invisible ball between my fingers and she asks me, What's inside the ball? But I don't get angry and I just tell her,

"Nothing." And she says, "Oh, nothing! I love nothing, it's the only thing that lasts forever."

Now did you ever hear anything that ever made more sense than that!

So I say to her:

"I'm gonna tell you something and I'm gonna ask you something and whatever you tell me that's what I'll do."

So I tell her:

"My mother is possessed by the devil, my father is the saddest man in the world, my sister is in love with a dog, the one I love does not love me, and I got no place to live. What should I do?"

Now she doesn't just jump in with some answer like "Join the Y!" No. She THINKS about it. And you can tell she's thinking because she gets that look of a wrinkled-up forehead and staring off at a spot that isn't there. They are putting the chairs on the tables at Denny's she's still thinking. We gotta leave, we're walking on the street she's still thinking about it. We gotta go back to her place, which is this sewer by the highway, well it's more like a tunnel... no, no, it's a sewer. So we're sitting there in the mouth of her sewer watching the trucks go by on the highway she's still thinking about it. Finally the sun's about to come up she gets up walks back to the middle of the sewer looks at me she's got this smile, she's gonna tell me what I should do. But then her smile that she's smiling keeps getting bigger across her whole face and it doesn't stop on her face, it keeps going right off her face, growing and growing and growing and fills up the whole inside of the sewer. Then, this smile it turns itself inside out and from inside the smile walk out all these people: Mary Ann, Millard, Andrew, Doris, my sister, my mother, my father, Stew, Darlene, Brenda, Tom, Dave the bishop, people, people, people, all the people I know and they are all wearing the smile of this girl and they are all smiling at me. *Then*, every one of these people they all turn into birds. Every different kind of bird. Normal little brown birds, pigeons, owls, parrots, eagles, birds of extinction, birds of storybooks, every different kind of bird, and then all these birds they all come over to me and put their claws in me—but not in my skin! Just in my clothes, in my jacket, in my pants, in my shoes, in my hair a little bit but not too hard... I've got a million wings, and then all these birds they lift me up and fly me right out of the sewer out over the highway over houses over trees over the MOUNTAINS over the OCEAN far, far away to this secret field that nobody knows exists—well some people know about it but it's very hard to get to—and they drop me down in the middle of this field and I fall asleep and I have this dream:

> *VICTOR picks up the clamp lamp, snaps his fingers, stage lights out, clamp lamp on.*

We're not in the theatre. We're not in the building. We're in this dream. And we're on a bus. Going north. To... Wadawhichawawa... (Wadawhichawawa!) It's very far north and we've never been there before and we don't know anybody there and that's why we're going. It's night, dark, all those little bus lights are on, some people are reading, some people are looking out the window, at the highway going by, trees moving, stars in the moonlight, animal eyes in the woods, dark, quiet. Then that woman at the front who bought the egg-salad sandwich at the pee break, she starts singing this song and we don't know it but we all start singing it too... well if we sing it I guess we know it...

This song:
(sings) Well I'm coming by tomorrow with a hacksaw and a hammer /
Gonna build a little place for you and me /
Be just the way we like it and we'll make sure that it's sturdy /
Gonna last a long, long time for you and me.

And then that sunny morning we will move into our castle /
Gonna keep the outside world from you and me /
And we'll wake up every morning with our arms around each other
and we'll walk into our kitchen and we'll hold our cups of coffee and
we'll look out of our window and how oh so very happy we will be /
We will be /
And how oh so very happy we will be, be, be /
Be...
Be...

VICTOR holds up the tiny invisible ball between his thumb
and forefinger. He brings his thumb and forefinger together.
Black.

HERE LIES HENRY

Here Lies Henry was developed in a workshop produced by da da kamera and Festival Antigonish in Antigonish, Nova Scotia.

Henry: Daniel MacIvor
Director: Daniel Brooks
Technical director: Ian Pygott
Producer: Sherrie Johnson for da da kamera
Producer: Addy Doucette for Festival Antigonish

Here Lies Henry was first produced by da da kamera as part of the Six Stages Festival at Buddies in Bad Times Theatre in Toronto, Ontario.

Henry: Daniel MacIvor
Director: Daniel Brooks
Lighting design: Andrea Lundy, Jan Komarek, and Andy Moro
Sound design: Richard Feren
Producer: Sherrie Johnson for Six Stages and da da kamera

This is a new version of this text, rewritten for the 2007 Toronto remount produced by Buddies In Bad Times Theatre and da da kamera.

NOTES TO FUTURE PRODUCTIONS

MUSIC AND SOUND

In the original productions Henry wore a microphone through which his voice was at times affected. Sound and music were also used often throughout the performance as an indication of a level of reality outside Henry's control. These moments are not notated in this text. Use your imagination.

LIGHT

The lighting in the original production consisted of a series of boxes that grew increasingly smaller until only Henry's face was lit. I have notated lighting changes in this text.

COSTUME

Henry should be dressed up, looking his best.

SET

A bare stage. In the front row of the audience is a chair which is clearly marked as reserved for a local dignitary. Perhaps the mayor. Someone whose presence is possible.

Performance

Henry is talking to this audience, tonight, in this space. Everything is happening now.

Text

There is a level of improvisation which happens with the audience, and I have noted these moments and given suggestions in parenthesis. Contemporary and local references should be altered and added to keep the production current and inside the local community. I have also noted where these alterations and additions might occur. Also, it would be out of character for Henry not to say, "Bless you," if someone in the audience should sneeze. And if a cellphone should ring he would certainly respond with an "I'm not here," or "Is that for me?"

Marketing

In presenting a production it might be in your best interests to downplay the role of the outside writer (me). If the audience is overtly conscious of a "writer" then it makes it difficult to look at the show as happening tonight. Perhaps keep mention of the writer off the posters and promo and only give credit in the show's program. Also, in the program Daniel Brooks must receive credit as dramaturge.

A dark stage. Now.
Ominous music.
HENRY enters through a dim tunnel of light.
HENRY coughs. Music out, light up bright.
HENRY regards the audience fearfully.
He smiles weakly.
More fear.
He nods hello to a couple of individuals.
HENRY knows he has to do something but he's not sure what.
HENRY has an idea.

HENRY

(singing, tentative) "Grab your coat and get your hat, leave your worries on the doorstep, life could be so sweet *(getting into it)* on the sunny side of the street!" *(He hits a bad note on the last word; he tries to find the right note.)* "...street." "...street." No. "...street." *(He can't find the note, he gives up.)*

He regards the audience fearfully.
He checks his fly.
He mimes a bird with his hands, it flies and lands on his shoulder.

An uncomfortable pause.

You don't want to get me started talking, I might never shut up.

I took a public slpeak...

I took a public-speaking course.

One: Don't say "um."

Two: Never apologize.

Three: Don't say "anyway."

Four: ...Um...?

Sorry.

Anyway. Ahhh!

It's hard.

I'm not prepared. Not that I didn't have time to prepare but... well you know how these things are. Or maybe you don't, I don't know.

Ah but what's preparation anyway? Just the mortal enemy of spontaneity. I've always had a problem being spontaneous—

No, that's a lie.

All right then, let's get Spontaneous!

He does a little dance.
After a moment he gives up.
He regards the audience.
He tries to think of something to say.

Oh... kay. A tourist in New York and the tourist walks up to a cab driver, and the tourist asks the cab driver: "Do you know where Carnegie Hall is?" and the cab driver says...

Oh.

That's wrong.

Or!

Why are fire engines red?

Because…!

Actually, my grandma told me that. It's kind of for kids. It's silly.

Or…

A podiatrist walks into a bar…. No, a proctologist…. Or.…

Usually I'm pretty good with…. But when you need one you just can't think of…

An uncomfortable pause.

I've got a place if you're looking. And who isn't? Everybody's always looking for a better…. Two bedrooms, hardwood floors, fireplace, view of the park, nine-fifty all-inclusive. It's a very good deal. Of course if you take it you'll have to contend with the body in the next room. Oooo, what's this suddenly? A mystery! *CSI: Me* suddenly.

Note: the price of the apartment should support current market and local trends as "a good deal." Also, the television program should be a current mystery-type program.

No.

I had the strangest dream.

Music and light shift: deeply eerie.

It wasn't that strange.

Music out and light restored.

An uncomfortable pause.

What ever happened to Nigel Kennedy? Remember him. With the violin? He was really... good. Edgy. I'm a little edgy. I'm doing a cold-turkey thing. Tried Nicorette, tried the patch, nothing works for me—just cold turkey. It takes time but—
Time! Oh you'll like this.
"A Brief Moment With Time."
(in a funny voice) Hi I'm Time!
(a different funny voice) Hi I'm Time!
(searching for the voice) Hi I'm Time!
I can't find the right.... I need a few drinks for that one. It's more of a party thing.

An uncomfortable pause.

See *CSI*?
You get *CSI* here?
The one with the girl? I hate that show. That girl's too thin. She's probably a vegetarian—

> *Note: This should be the same television program mentioned earlier. We can safely assume any television program of this ilk will feature a too-thin female.*

OH! Okay, this is good:
I'm in the salad bar, upstairs there's some vegetarian symposium or something going on. Have you ever been in an all-you-can-eat salad bar with a room full of vegetarians? No wonder they don't eat pigs, they are pigs!

A moment as he takes in the audience reaction.

I didn't mean to offend any vegetarians.
But you should have seen when they brought out the nutloaf!
"Oooo the nutloaf. Have you tried the nutloaf? The nutloaf is gorgeous! Oh the nutloaf! Forget the bean dip try the nutloaf! Come on everybody gather round the nutloaf!"
Do I have to listen to this much longer?

An uncomfortable pause.
He regards the audience fearfully.

Is this right?
Is this what you expected?
Is this what I'm supposed to do?
Is this what you wanted?
Is this why I came all this way?
Would you love me... if I let you?
Does it matter?
Does anything?

An uncomfortable pause.

Good evening.
I am here to tell you something you don't already know. Maybe you knew that already, I don't know.
I am here—good—to tell you something—yes—that you don't already know— Exactly!
My name is.... My name! Well some of you may know my name but for those of you who don't—is Henry "Tom" Gallery. Gallery yes gallery like gallery yes. Gallery.

Big deal so what. What's in a name?
Ten-and-a-half shoe.
Fifteen-and-a-half neck.
Thirty-one-inch waist—thirty-two—thirty-three.

Note: the above sizes should suit the actor.

And I would consider myself, if I was supposed to consider myself, at knifepoint or gunpoint or some point something, I would consider myself a *bon viv*— No.
A man of the— No.
A lousy— No.
A…. An optimist!
I would consider myself an optimist.
Of course to say that one is an optimist is just to say that one is a liar. I mean just look around. The more of an optimist one tries to be the bigger the liar one must become. I mean just look around.

Although I was probably a liar before I was an optimist. You see my father *(cough)* sorry. My father *(short cough)* sorry. My father *(cough)* my father *(cough)* my father *(cough)*. Sorry. My father *(cough)*'s name was Henry. But everyone called him Tom. Because his father's name was Tom and everyone thought he should have been named after his father so everyone called him Tom even though his name was Henry. I was named after my father *(cough)* sorry. Henry. But since no one called him Henry and everyone called him Tom everybody called me Tom even though my name was—is *(singing)* ta dah! Henry. And I came to understand at a very early age that not only was my name a lie but I was a liar.

Nietzsche said *(sneeze)*: "Lies are necessary to life and this is part and parcel of the questionable and horrible nature of existence." Honey!

An uncomfortable pause.

It's very easy to be a liar when—when one is a—one is a small child because then one is just said to have an "overactive imagination"—which is to say that if one were to... oh, I don't know say... lock the babysitter in the bathroom and run around the house yelling "Fire!" well, that wouldn't really be a lie, that would just be an overactive imagination. But of course it's a lie. You can't hide a lie like fire, I know I've been there, there's evidence: singed shingles, bits of melted plastic, ashen diaries, burnt words, smoking three-string violins, so on. Of course... out of guilt out of having lied about the fire one might... set a fire. But then one would be an arsonist. And once one is an arsonist that pretty much overrides whether or not one is a liar. Or even an optimist for that matter.

My mother *(short laugh)* was an optimist. "Grab your coat and get your hat" ...Even when the house burnt down... "Leave your worries on the doorstep" ...The first thing she said was... "Life could be so sweet" ...Well at least now we can move to... "The sunny side of the street" ...That was her favourite song. My mother *(laugh)*. She was a nurse... ran a restaurant on the side. And my father *(cough)* sorry, was an army man. I was conceived on the evening of June the fourth. I was an only child. This disturbed my sister quite a bit. And I had a dog named Betty. Betty. With a "y." Not an "e." That would be Bette. Betty with a "y." There was a girl on our street named

Betty, she thought the dog was named after her but it wasn't it was just named after… nothing; it was just named after… itself. Betty. "Betty, Betty, come for dinner!" That's… what we'd call… when it was… time for… the… dog to… come to dinner…. Sometimes the girl would come…. She might get a sandwich…. Or a bowl of cereal maybe.

And other than that…. Just more of the… you know… regular stuff…. Yup.

And that about does it. Me in a nutshell. Yup. *(singing)* Ta dah. *(He looks at a spot on the inside of his forearm.)* Gawd!

He regards the audience fearfully. He might cry. He pulls it together.

I love Scrabble!

And I don't cheat.

Unless someone else is cheating. But then that's not cheating is it, that's just changing the rules.

And I asked for a Scrabble dictionary every Christmas for the past ten years and do you think I got one?

"Nice sweater."

"Thanks for the pen."

A moment. HENRY becomes defiant.

And I don't believe in God.

He has second thoughts about being defiant.

Well I used to—I did when—I don't now…

Should I?

Why am I asking you? Let's just say I'm conflicted. I read his book. I didn't really "get it." I liked that Noah thing—that was good, but that first story. This is something I've thought about. The Garden? I mean really. Ladies? A rib? Do you want fries with that rib? I mean, what does it mean? I mean, they say it means something about knowledge and good and evil but, I mean, to me it seems to mean: the truth will make you naked. I mean, look at it. What have you got? You've got Adam and Evelyn in the Garden. Birds, trees, flowers, the silver moon, the blue lagoon, bliss. Ah Bliss! And then along comes the guy in the green suit and the snakeskin boots and the oh-oh tree and "Oh-oh it's the apple." And a nibble nibble later and there stands Truth in the once blissful now raging, now thundering garden. And what does Truth say? Truth does not say "Goodtaseeya!" Truth does not say, "That, sir, is a very nice shirt." Truth says: "You people are naked!"

You people are naked.

So if now is now and this: *(covers his genitals with his hands)* is Truth well, what was then and Bliss? You see? If on one hand you've got Truth and then on the other hand you've got Bliss— and if that's the choice, hey, I'll take Bliss. Hey I'll take two!
That's my thesis thank you.
Whatever.

He loosens up. He dances a bit. The Swim. The Hitchhiker.

Let's have some music; let's have some fun!

Nothing happens.

Perhaps now's not the time.

He boldly regards the audience.

Good evening!
My name is Henry "Tom" Gallery. The second.
And I am a liar.
And if we're going to talk about me—and that seems to be the point—then we are going to talk about lies, and if we're going to talk about lies then you are in very good hands.
All right.
Now it is very important to understand the Art of Lying. There are many—there are uncountab—there are eight types of lies, and the first type of lie is… the Just Kidding Lie.
Now, in order to demonstrate the Just Kidding Lie I am going to need a volunteer.

He approaches a member of the audience. He speaks to this person directly.

Just kidding.

He returns to the stage.

Just Kidding!

Now the second type of lie is… the White Lie. Now, the White Lie is told to keep another from harm or deep embarrassment, or to ingratiate one's self. For example: "No, I don't mind putting my dog down." Well, that's a bit obscure. How about: "What a beautiful baby."

The next type of lie is the Lie Lie or The Excuse. Now the Lie Lie is very easy to perceive because it is accompanied by sweaty palms, darting eyes and incomplete sentences such as: "I-was-just-I-was-just-I-don't-know-why-the-house-burnt-down-Gawd!" The Lie Lie is used on parents, teachers, bosses, creditors. The success of the Lie Lie depends entirely on the Lie-ee's desire to believe the Lie-er. Works almost never in the case of creditors, almost always in the case of parents.

The next type of lie is the Pathological Lie. Now the Pathological Lie is a very interesting type of lie, tied up with problems with self-esteem—messy things like that. Advantages of pathological lying include: fame and fortune, great at a party, fabulous resumé! Disadvantages of pathological lying include: bad credit rating, time in the slammer, madness.

> *He laughs a ridiculous, mad laugh. The audience reaction throws him.*

The next type of lie is the...

> *He stops, having lost his thought. (The "you" following can be the audience as a whole or an individual.)*

Oh look now you've got me lost ...
I'm not angry I'm just disappointed.
OH. Right. Lucky for you. The Professional Lie. Now the Professional Lie is best left to be explained by those who prac-

tise this lie: politicians, lawyers, general contractors, dental hygienists, botanists, urban planners, farmers, tailors, podiatrists, psychics, engineers, members of the clergy, the military, and the royal family.

The next type of lie is the Survival Lie or the Lie To Survive. Now this is a complex and anti-mathematical condition where deep belief in the lie manifests the desired outcome. Deep belief in the lie manifests the desired outcome. Such as "I love you." Or "It Will Be Better In The Morning."

And the next type of lie—the final type of lie—is the Universal Lie. Now the Universal Lie is almost impossible to talk about because we all share it. The Universal Lie is also known as Time.

> *Silence as he looks at the audience.*
> *He turns away, his back to the audience.*
> *Sound: building rain and then a thunderstorm.*
> *Light: slow fade to near black.*
> *(This sound and light should take at least thirty seconds.)*
> *He turns back to the audience suddenly.*
> *Sound and light restore.*

You know… I have a feeling. And I have a feeling that: we're a lot alike. It's simple… it's obvious… it's just the nature of existence. One, two, three.

One, you're born.

Two, you assume… yes… a series of—I don't know—experiences.

Three, you die.

One, you're born: dark passage into a bright room.

Two, you assume... yes... a series of—I don't know—experiences:

You learn to walk.

You learn to talk.

You have your first day of school.

You get a dog, or a cat, or a gerbil, or a turtle: it runs away or dies.

You can't wait for Christmas, or Hanukkah, or Ramadan or what have you.

You collect things: matchbooks, Boy Scout badges, cardboard.

You enter puberty and spend two fabulous years in your bedroom with James Taylor.... Or Carly Simon or whatever the case may be.

> *Note: The above musicians should be singer/songwriter types active during the adolescence of the actor playing HENRY.*

You get your driver's licence.

You leave home.

You never write, but you call!

You think about going to college and you don't, or you do.

You lose your ideals and drift aimlessly toward the void.

Until! You meet your love in a laundromat or at a party. You take that wonderful walk you make that perfect promise. Or! You convince yourself that some people just weren't meant to couple.

But either way you seize the day, you change your mind, you make a plan, you resolve to stop, to start, to seize the day to change your mind to make a plan. You, in short, experience.

Three, you die: bright passage into a dark room. *(stretching out his arm toward the audience and making a circle which grows faster and faster and smaller and smaller)* Dark passage into a bright room, experience, experience, experience, bright passage into a dark room. Dark passage into a bright room, bright passage into a dark room, dark passage into a bright room, bright passage into a dark room, bright into a dark, dark into a bright into a dark into bright into dark into bright.

And that's the hook and here's the catch and the catch of the day is sole. And the bone that runs down the middle, from which grows the fillet, the spine of the soul, is Hope.

And of course there's always hope.

Of course, there's always hope!

Of course, there's always hope?

And of course you have hope.

But that is where we differ.

He smiles weakly. He wipes sweat from his forehead.

Let's have some music; let's have some fun!

Music: In the original production we used "Finally" by CeCe Peniston—but whatever choice it should be the song he refers to in the final segment when HENRY tells us his favourite song.

Whoo!

Light: a dance club.
He dances with mad delight.

Whoo!

Sound and light restore.

I understand there's a lot of vegetarians in the room tonight. The only thing better than a room full of vegetarians is a room full of vegetarians at an all-you-can-eat salad bar. "Ooooo that nutloaf, oooo that nutloaf, gimme that nutloaf, gimme that nutloaf, gimme that nutloaf." Do I have to listen to you people fuck that nutloaf much longer?
Whoo!

Music and light: nightclub.
He dances with mad delight.

Whoo!

Sound and light restore.

Why are fire engines red?
Because two and two is four and four and four are eight and eight and four is twelve and twelve inches is a ruler and a ruler could be queen and the queen's name could be Mary and *Queen Mary* is the name of a ship and ships sail over the ocean and fishes swim in the ocean and fishes have fins and the Finns fought the Russians and Russians are always red and fire engines are always rushin'.
Oh that's silly, Russians aren't even Russian anymore.
Whoo!

Music and light: nightclub.
He dances with mad delight.

Whoo!

Sound and light restore.

How do I get to Carnegie Hall?
Practise!
What a shitty mood I'm in tonight you lucky fuckers!
Whoo!

Music and light: nightclub.
He dances with mad delight.

Whoo!

Sound and light restore.

Did I mention the body in the next room?
Who thought "poofter"? Who thought "poofter"?
Oh, that was me!
Whoo!

Music and light: nightclub.
He dances with mad delight.
Sound and light slowly restore.

Remember that fire I said I set before? Oh, I didn't say I set it, did I? Never mind.

A small jeté.

This is fun.
Okay I talked about the Garden, should I talk about the Flood?

He bows deeply.

Thank you.

So what else about me?

Let's see! Well my father *(cough)* sorry, was a pack of Benson and Hedges Special Lights and my mother *(laugh)* was a fried-egg sandwich. I was conceived on the evening of June the fourth, I remember it well. It was a rainy evening, and she with her legs pressed tightly together, but not tightly enough, and he pries them apart and a couple of drunken pumps later and the sperm hits the egg and ta dah! Oh if only every night could be like that.

I was an only child, as I said this disturbed my sister quite a bit, but as it turned out she wasn't really my sister she was really my mother. *(laugh)* But I bet nobody wants to talk about that though, do they? And I had a dog named Betty, for dinner, she was delicious. Ba dum bum!

At the age of nine I had a religious vision which turned out to be not a religious vision at all just something I ate. This disappointed my mother *(laugh)* quite a bit because she always wanted to have a visionary son and instead she just got a comment on her cooking. Which it was. She only had one dish. Fried-egg sandwiches. Not that they weren't stupendous fried-egg sandwiches. I'm sure it's the only reason my father *(cough)* stayed with my mother. *(laugh)* Unfortunately sixteen hundred fried-egg sandwiches later he died. Heart attack. We found him on the floor of the billiards room—no, the conservatory—or the library? He didn't have a clue! Didn't help that he was an alka-alka-alcoholic. He started his own group actually, Happy Alcoholics. H.A. HA! Group worked out quite well at first although I don't think they should have met in a bar.

BA DUM BUM! At the age of eleven I had to make an important life-changing decision between playing either the violin or rugby. Being a homosexual—

He regards the audience.

And I bet you knew that already, bet you could tell, my father *(cough)* sorry, certainly could. Or perhaps you don't care, my mother *(laugh)* certainly did. Or perhaps you're thinking: "Gee I wish I could take him downtown to a cheap hotel and drown him in sloppy kisses and make long, hot, horny love to him until the sun is high in the afternoon sky!" ...Perhaps not. My lover certainly didn't. *(weeps a moment then pulls himself out of it)* But! Being a homosexual and having to choose between either rugby or the violin I did what any good young homosexual would do and I chose... rugby!

I played often to the delight of many.

The next year I was diagnosed as being dyslexic but it turned out I wasn't really dyslexic at all, I was really ambidextrous. Which is a good thing. The left hand knows what the right hand does. I'm good with my hands. See? *(He mimes a bird.)* I'm good with birds.

Oh stop that!

Lived in a house. Indeed. Watched it burn to the ground. Very traumatic. And, as I said, my mother *(laugh)* was a podiatrist and my father *(cough)* worked—managed a brewery—or.... And other than that, it was just a sort of idyllic sort of miserable sort of storybook sort of nightmarish sort of remarkable sort of regular sort of existence. One thing was I managed to graduate from high school by the age of thirteen, but what's that really though just intelligence, not even intelligence really, there was a nine-year-old in my graduating class, speaks more about the program than it does about my intelligence, but what's intelligence anyway huh? Can't pay the rent with it. Can't date it. *(weeps for a moment and then quickly pulls himself out of it)* And I told you about the thing I had with James Taylor. *(Note: same musician as puberty obsession)* Well I also had a thing with Elizabeth Taylor and I also had a thing with Karen Black, remember her? And I was the guy who blew coke up Stevie Nicks's ass.

> *Note: it is important that HENRY remain a contemporary with the audience and so if there should come a time when Elizabeth Taylor, Karen Black, or Stevie Nicks would not have been alive during Henry's lifetime the Elizabeth Taylor comment can be altered to any aging screen goddess who might have a perfume (re: the final segment), the Karen Black comment can be altered to any Hollywood actress who performed an amazing feat in an action movie while wearing a skirt, and the Stevie Nicks comment can be altered to any off-colour rock-and-roll myth.*

Sorry.
Anyway.
Sorry.
Sorry. Um. Sorry. Anyway. Um.   Anyway. Um. Sorry. Sorry. Sorry. Um. Anyway.

> *This continues for at least twenty seconds. HENRY gets caught in not being able to say anything but these three words in various successions. He stops himself and he does a little yoga to try and relax. He relaxes. He takes a breath.*

Anyway. AHHHHHH!

And I'm a prince! Sounds far-fetched—not really, went to Spain, ran with some royals, bit of a scandal, had to leave, can't talk about it. And I was in the crash upon which *Airport 75* was based. Well, I wasn't actually *in* the crash but I had reservations which I cancelled at the very last second.

> *Note: The* Airport 75 *comment can be altered to the name of the action movie in which the above Hollywood actress replacing Karen Black appeared. For example, one might replace Karen Black in the earlier segment with Sigourney Weaver. In that case the line above would be "And I was on the spaceship upon which* Aliens *was shot. Well I wasn't actually on the spaceship but I had reservations which I cancelled at the very last second." Use your imagination. The point is that HENRY shouldn't be reaching for past events or personalities outside the lifetime of the actor playing HENRY.*

And I become a commercial pilot but I couldn't take the job because it turned out that I was too tall. Then I ran for public office, and I won! But I couldn't take that job either because I'm allergic to air conditioning. So I went to California and got involved in the porn industry under the name Prince McLaine. Perhaps you've seen one of my tapes? The most successful was called "Oh Yeah, Oh Yeah, Oh I'm A Bad Boy, Oh I'm A Bad Boy, Oh That's A Big One, Oh That's A Big One, Give The Bad Boy The Big One, Give The Bad Boy The Big One, Oh Yeah, Oh Yeah, Oh No, Oh No, Oh Yeah, Oh Yeah, HOOOOLLLLLEEEEE!" Google that you'll be up all night. Then I went to prison and I wrote a book based on my experience there which you've probably read because it was a bestseller but I had to use a pseudonym because I'm part of the witness protection program— Oh shit! Forget I said that!

Then I suffered—ha—studied years with the Ernst-Phelps-Greens, famous for their seminal work *The Doors of Deception* ta dah! And it is from this work whence I take my axiom, which is: "When the rose smells sweet the rose smells sweet, when the rose is dead THE ROSE SMELLS SWEET!" Words to live by. I'm a little edgy. I'm doing a cold-turkey thing. Tried Nicorette tried the patch nothing works for me—just cold turkey. It takes time but—TIME! Time, there's one! Time! You'll love this! "Hi how ya doin. Time." A brief moment with Time! "Hey how ya doin I'm Time. Nice shirt. I like to go go go I don't want any of this stop and smell the roses bullshit. If I wanted patience I would have been a dentist." Beeeeeautiful teeth. Beauty, there's another one. Time and Beauty. They share a place together you know. Oh yes they do. Two bedrooms, hardwood floors, fireplace, view of the park, nine-fifty all-inclusive. It's a very good deal. But Beauty just doesn't "get" Time. And Time loathes Beauty because she's so smug! All she does is sit around all day and drink decaffeinated cappuccino after decaffeinated cappuccino and plan the colours for the sunset. So Time decides he's going to kill Beauty but he realizes he has to be very clever about it so he sets her on fire. But it is a very special fire that burns very slowly and doesn't have a flame. But Beauty realizes "sumthin's up" so she goes to see Hope but all Hope can do is give her a placebo and that's really too bad because a placebo only works if you believe in it and sweetheart, Beauty don't believe in nuthin but herself. Oh yeah! Been there!

After a moment.

69

And then I suffered—ha—studied for many years with the Ernst-Phelps-Greens famous for their seminal work *The Doors of Deception* ta dah. Oh I said that already.

And I wrote a paper for them! Yes, I did! A radical scholastic revisionism of the flood. The Noah thing? Perhaps you've heard of my paper? "The Water Is Wide I Cannot Cross O'r"? No? Good!

All right. It's the flood. And you're on the ark. The rain was over long, you know, ago, and you're on the ark. You and two of every living animal. The ark's not that big and it's probably leaking, but nobody wants to talk about that I bet do they? And you're wandering on the deck one day and you see that stupid goat chewing on a branch and you think, "Oh that stupid goat, always—" and you think, "Wait a minute, duh, where did the goat get the branch?" It's the flood right? And then you see that stupid bird on the rail and you think, "Oh the goat just took the branch from the stupid bird—" And then you think, "Wait a minute, duh, where did the bird get the branch?" It's the flood, right? So you go and you take the branch from the stupid goat.... "Gimme that." And you take the branch to your father *(cough)* sorry, and he recognizes the significance of the branch. And of course he takes credit for the whole fucking thing himself. But who's to judge right? And then he calls a branch symposium down in the common room and we're all gathered down in the common room and up pops Pop on the table and he holds the branch up over his head, just like this, like so, nothing too dramatic, just like this, over his head.

And we all look at the branch and we think: "Well if there's a branch then there must be a tree, and if there's a tree there must be soil, and if there's soil there must be a hole, and if there's a hole there must be a foundation, and if there's a foundation there must be a house, and if there's a house there must be rooms, and if there are rooms there must be closets and drawers and cupboards and boxes and stores and three daily newspapers and all the stuff that goes in 'em, and the body in the next room and me in my comfortable chair in front of my HDTV surrounded by a limitless, boundless, endless sea of the most profound... inertia.

So much for hope.

Downer.

I wish I had my violin. I'd play it. I bet you didn't think I could play the violin but not only was I a star on the rugby field and a member of the Olympic Bowling Team but I was also a *(name of local music competition)* winner.
Runner-up.
Worked the coat check.
I couldn't play it anyway though it only has three strings.
(burp) Ooo. Nutloaf.

We could talk about television but I don't watch television. Very much. Well, CBC of course, who doesn't. And PBS—for arty stuff. And CNN to keep informed. And once in awhile CTV, or Global. In a pinch maybe ABC. And NBC for fun. And CBS for *CSI*. And now and then MSNBC or TLN or TLC or CMT—but not for the music. And for movies sometimes Showcase or Bravo and HBO but that's not really TV, it's HBO. And who can live without Home Shopping. And if it's really late and the cable's out snow can be calming.

Note: Obviously the above should be current and all of the stations mentioned should be recognizable to the audience. Use your imagination.

That's a very nice shirt.
I noticed that before.
You're welcome.
That's a very nice shirt too.
Perhaps you two should have a Shirt-Off.
That's a very nice shirt too.
Thanks for making an effort.

Note: HENRY is speaking to individuals in the audience, but please do not feel a need to light the audience in order for the actor playing HENRY to be able to see them. The actor can use his imagination. The actor may not be able to see the individuals but HENRY can.

Of course there's always love.

Music: a soft samba.
He dances, oblivious to the audience.
Suddenly he notices them watching him.

What?

He continues to dance.
He notices the audience once again.

What?! Stop it.

He continues to dance.
He notices the audience.
He teasingly flirts and then stops, smiling mischievously.

Stop it.
What are you thinking?

He begins to dance openly with the audience.
He raises his hand over his head and brings it down in a stab-
bing motion which he repeats over and over with increasing,
grinning rage.
The music cuts in and out with the stabbing until it disap-
pears completely.

Light has shifted since the beginning of the music so that we
are now in a smaller playing space.

Ah love.
Love is lovely. Yes it is. Well you should know. So should
I. Because we're in love. Yes we are. You and Me. I'm me,
obviously. You're you. You have an overbite, which I find cute.
You have a love of crossword puzzles, which I am willing to
overlook. You have an allergy to my dog, so I put her down.
Why? Because this is love. This is something real something yes
something now something true something oh my God something beyond you and me.

The only thing is, we haven't met yet. It's inevitable that we
shall meet, it's just the method that needs to be settled upon.
So, I decide what I'm going to do to meet you is I'm going to
have a parade!

But have you ever tried to have a parade? The red tape, I must have made eighty-six phone calls, and all the pressure I just would have started drinking again and that would have been a book of rejection.

So, I decide what I'm going to do to meet you is rent a hall, get an outfit, invite some people. But try getting that together. Everybody's got their schedule everybody's got their favourite caterer.

So, I decide what I'm going to do to meet you is I'm going to dig a hole and I'm going to climb in and I'm going to sit there and I'm going to wait for you to walk by. And so I do. And I wait and I wait and I wait, and of course you don't walk by and of course it rains and of course I don't have a change of clothes and I have to go and sit in a laundromat in my underwear and wait for my clothes to dry... and as Fate would have it: you walk in. And of course you don't look at me because you're trained not to look at people in landromats in their underwear. But I look at you. And not only do I look at you but I see you: and your overbite and your chewed-up pencil and your cute little mm mm mm mm mmmmm and the stupid look on your face when your sock hits the floor and I think, "It might be," and your reaction when the hot zipper hits your forearm... *(He looks at a spot on the inside of his forearm.)* Gawd! ...and I think: It is.

And then you look at me, but you don't see me, and then you leave and I promise that I will meet you again. And I do. At a party. And at first it's a little uncomfortable, but then we take that wonderful walk, through the garden. And the trees are green with envy because we're so perfect. And the moon is blue with sadness because now we're taken. And we make our vow. Our promise:

I promise... I swear on my empty heart and my overworked liver, on my fallen arches and my bashful kidney, that I may fall and I may stumble and I may take you down with me. I may drink until I'm numb and spend entire nights with my head in the toilet. I may give you many, many days of despair. I may hate your family. I may miss your birthday. I may forget to call, be late for dinner, and not show up until sometime the next afternoon. I may betray you. With your friends. Publicly. I may degrade myself in order to win an argument. I may become only more sour and only more cynical and only more stubborn and when I die you may wish me one more moment of feeling if only but to slap me in the face. But I swear on my empty heart and my overworked liver, on my failing, flailing, falling body, that it is only ever—has only ever been, will only ever be—me for you and you for me.

Now, that's love.

But then of course there's life to contend with. And Reality with her alarm-clock earrings. And that weekend in Niagara Falls when we meet Doubt in the bar. And that night we invite Reason to stay over. And that day we discover that all along our landlord had been Compromise.... But poor old Compromise given the bad rap of meaning failure when in fact Compromise is Love's best friend.

But of course Time passes and Beauty, unaware, burns and what was once the perfect match, the perfect spark, the perfect flame, the perfect match of...? White and white. Now becomes sugar and salt. So that from a distance: white and white. But try one in soup and the other in tea and you will see how different white from white can be. So where does that leave us?

I'll tell you where.

I'm in the kitchen. You're in the living room. You call out, "Where are you?" and I call out, "I'm in the kitchen." But you can't hear me so you call out, "Where are you?" and I call out, "I'm in the kitchen." But you can't hear me so you call out, "Where are you?" and I call out, "I'm in the kitchen." But you can't hear me and I think: "Yes you can, yes you can so hear me. You just want me to come, you just want me to come like a dog. Well you're allergic to dogs—why do you want me to act like one." And you call out, "Where are you?" and I call out, "I'M IN THE FUCKING KITCHEN, YOU FUCK!!"

You come into the kitchen, you say, "What was all that about?"

I say: "I, am, in, the, kitchen!"

You say: "Well why didn't you just tell me?"

I say: "I did!"

You say: "Well you didn't have to yell."

Now. What can I do then?

Well, I can do two things: "A" or "B."

"A":

I can stab you twenty-seven times with a bread knife. Twenty-eight counting zero.

And when I do I think three things, and the first thing I think is: "I guess that psychic was right when she told me to stay away from sharp objects." And the second thing I think is, "That was sooooo easy." And the third thing I think is, "Well, I guess I can't argue now when people say I've got a temper." But isn't that a good thing to be able to admit you've got a temper?

Of course I do think other things but they're all "psychological" and I h-h-hate psychology because psychology says that people were meant to be understood and if people were meant to be understood you'd come with a tag behind your ear, they'd run credits at funerals.

Or "B":

I can go into the living room, sit in my comfortable chair in front of my HDTV and continue to hate you.

And when I do, I reach down, deep down inside myself and I take out that tiny sharp-edged shrapnel of hope, that we all have lodged within us from the big explosion, and I press it, hard, between my index fingers, until the warm red is running down my arms, dripping off my elbows, and staining the carpet on either side of the chair.

But either way, "A" or "B," it's a bucket of blood, and where does that leave us with our love reduced to being nothing but... "the body in the next room."

And of course it has to be somebody's fault, it always does. And of course it's my fault, it always is. It always comes down to me. Yes that's right, I lost your keys, on purpose. I came home early from holiday, intentionally, so I could catch you in bed with that idiot, how uncomfortable was that, I'm so sorry. You give and you give and you give and you give and you give and I take take take take take take take take take. Because I am the monster. That's right. I'm the monster. I did it all. I take responsibility for everything. All of it. I rang your doorbell and ran away. That was me. I farted and said it was you, Grandpa! I did that too! And I charged you extra for that work I did on your house because I saw you had a nice car. And I told your husband that you were not, in fact, having lunch with your sister, and I was happy when I heard about the divorce. And when you got that new job and moved away I wished you the worst because I was jealous. And I pointed out the way to Anne Frank's hiding place because she made fun of me at school. And I started a war just so you could warm up your car on those cold winter mornings. And I put the phosphates in detergent so you could get your whites whiter than white. You're welcome. And I told Karen Carpenter she was fat because she said I couldn't sing. And I invented economics just to fuck you up. And I gave Karla and Paul the video camera for Christmas because they seemed so sweet. And I got JonBenet into pageants because you had to have something to watch on TV. And I taught Mohammed Atta how to fly a plane because New York thinks it's so fucking great!

Note: After "economics" please feel free to add more or other atrocities. "Karla and Paul" were notorious Canadian serial killers—a bounty of locally known to your audience are unfortunately available, I'm sure. The final atrocity should be recent and possibly just over the line of good taste.

Well... that's enough about me.
How about you?

He regards the audience until they are silent.

You're so quiet.

Note: If the audience does not become silent—perhaps they are laughing, or one person might say something disparaging, then HENRY would say "Exactly."

Well.
So much for love.

He looks away. He wipes, rubs his face.

Let's have some music. Let's have some fun!

Sound: ominous.

That's not exactly what I had in mind.

I don't know what the rules are but I think I'm just gonna have to break 'em.

He squints past the lights, regarding the audience carefully.

You know what I could really use about now?
Starts with a "C."
Ends with an "igarette."

He leaves the stage and approaches the audience.
He improvises something like:

Could I please have a cigarette? Hello? I'm not going to smoke it, I quit. I'm just going to hold it. It's just a comfort type thing. I couldn't smoke it anyway, that would be against the law! I know nobody actually smokes but sometimes people carry them just to be nice. I won't make you do anything, I just want to borrow a cigarette.

When someone gives him a cigarette:

Could you do one thing? Could you light it for me too? Just for the burning-ember feeling. I'm not going to smoke it, I quit. I wouldn't light it myself, it's like when you see an old lover, you might shake hands but you wouldn't hug.

When someone lights the cigarette for him he thanks them and takes the cigarette. As he returns to the stage he notices the chair reserved for the local dignitary.

Who's that reserved for? That fucker's not showing up.

He takes the chair and the cigarette and returns to the stage. He places the chair carefully on two spike marks on the stage.

I wondered what these little marks were for. I could have been sitting down the whole fucking time.

He stands in front of the chair.
If he is wearing a jacket he takes it off and throws it theatrically aside.

Don't get your hopes up, mister. Just Kidding.

If he is wearing a tie he takes it off.
He regards the cigarette.

That is so tempting.

He takes a long hard drag of the cigarette, inhaling deeply.

I didn't inhale.

He exhales into his shirt.
He speaks to the audience member who gave him a cigarette.

It's all your fault.

Note: If cigarette smoking becomes illegal in public to the
point of being a criminal offence and you don't want to take
the risk of a fine or imprisonment the above can be performed
as the following:

I don't know what the rules are but I think I'm just gonna
have to break 'em.

He squints past the lights regarding the audience carefully.
He notices the chair reserved for the local dignitary.
He approaches the chair.

Who's that reserved for? That fucker's not showing up.

He takes the chair and returns to the stage.
He places the chair carefully on two spike marks on the stage.

I wondered what these little marks were for. I could have
been sitting down the whole fucking time.

He stands in front of the chair.
If he is wearing a jacket he takes it off and throws it theatri-
cally aside.

Don't get your hopes up, mister. Just Kidding.

If he is wearing a tie he takes it off.

After a moment.

Let's get preposterous.

Light: a much smaller playing area.

Say the trees had eyes instead of leaves. Preposterous.

Say the sky was red red red and shut out all the sun. Preposterous.

Say cats had fangs and flew. Say the ocean boiled. Preposterous.

Say you had two little men, one on each shoulder, and each one was yelling into your ear in a different language that you didn't understand. Preposterous.

Say they sold you something at the corner store that would kill you but they wouldn't let you take your own life. Preposterous.

Say every time you went to take a step the ground opened up in front of you. Preposterous.

Say you're in a dark room, a wet room, a tight room, ahead of you is a tunnel, at the end of the tunnel a light, suddenly you are forced through the tunnel into the light, you're surrounded by people in green, little white masks, there's a woman there she's screaming, she's crying, she's laughing, you're covered in blood, lifted by the ankles, slapped on the bottom.

How can we get anymore preposterous than the way we came to be?

He sits.

Say you wake up, you have a bite, you watch some TV, you go out, you sit in front of a computer or you stand behind a counter, you go home, you watch some TV, you have a bite, you go to sleep.

Say you have the strangest dream...

You are lying in the remains of a burnt-out house in a field surrounded by singed shingles, bits of melted plastic, ashen diaries, burnt words, smoking three-string violins, so on, and beside you is a telephone and it is ringing but you can't answer it because you can't move. Then at the edge of the field a woman appears. She's dressed as a nurse, she's not a nurse but she's dressed as a nurse, and slowly she crosses the field and approaches the ringing telephone. Then she lifts the receiver and holds it to your ear and a man's voice on the other end says, "Water boils. Ice melts. Birds fly south."

Water boils. Ice melts. Birds fly south.

Well, tell me something I don't already know!

Say you wake up, you watch some TV, you have a bite, you try to go out, but you can't, you have a bite, you watch some TV, you go to sleep.

Say you wake up, you try to go out, but you can't, you try to have a bite, but you can't, you try to watch some TV, but you can't, you try to go to sleep, but you can't. So you lie there and look out the window at the rain, at the rain, at the rain. And then finally, very tired, you fall into what might be called a sleep, and then quite unremarkably unsuddenly and after much hanging on and many false alarms say... you die.

I'm a little edgy. I'm doing a cold-turkey thing. I tried Nicorette, I tried the patch. Nuthin' works for me just cold turkey. It takes time but.... Time—there's one, our old friend time...

Why are fire engines red?

Because: two and two is four. And four and four is eight. And eight and four is twelve. And twelve inches is... a ruler. And a ruler could be a queen. And the queen's name could be Mary. And *Queen Mary* is the name of a ship. And ships sail over the ocean. And fishes swim in the ocean. And fishes have fins. And Finns fought the Russians. And Russians are always red. And fire engines are always rushin'. Ba dum bum.

I like that.

Because it's a perfect little, endless little world.

Well it's not endless, it has a punchline. Or no... not a punchline. It's a riddle. Jokes have punchlines. Riddles have... something else... reasons.

But everything ends. Jokes end. Riddles end.

Everything ends.

And you can always see it coming.

In your face in the mirror, in a feeling in your stomach, in the strangest dream.

And because we can see it coming that is why we run. We do. I did. Running and running and running and I'm not so so many years old and I feel poisoned and I'm running and I'm running and I'm running and I'm running and I try to take a breath but the air is so thick that when I do I have to chew on it and it tastes sharp and sour. And running and running, and I try to think about tomorrow but tomorrow seems as far away as the sound of a marble rolling down a hill in an oil drum. And I'm running and I'm running and I trip over Time lying drunk on the sidewalk and I crash into Beauty begging for quarters beside a broken telephone booth, a piece of glass in her arm *(He looks at a spot on the inside of his forearm; if he is smoking he would drop the cigarette now.)* Gawd!

And running and running and running and I look up at a second-floor window and I see Reason and Compromise toasting Doubt and I'm running and I'm running and the cats are flying and crashing into the eyeball leaves of trees and the wind is spinning up fishbone tornadoes and the sky is red red red over the boiling ocean and the volcanoes are popping up like blackheads on a Boy Scout's back and the ground opens up in front of me and I fall through and as I fall I shatter into a million pieces but the pieces will not separate they are held together by the tiny magnet of my mind—crashing crashing crashing—and I land in the centre of my soul just in time to see all my houses burning burning burning and the walls collapse and the roofs cave in and the smoke pours out into the sky as full and easy as drunken promises, and I stand there and I wait and I watch until there is nothing left, not a single singed shingle not an ashen diary not a burnt word not a three-string violin not a nice shirt not a sunny day not a bad night not a good reason not a wish not a hope not a fear not a tear not a whisper not a whimper not a nothing not a nothing not a nothing not a nothing whimper not a nothing not a nothing not a nothing not a nothing whimper not a nothing not a nothing not a nothing not a nothing nothing nothing nothing...

Of course one might choose to stop running. And if one did then one would look down the dark and one might choose to go. And if one did, choose to go, then one would take you with them. One would. Take you. Everyone does, grandmothers, teenagers, movie stars, soldiers. Whenever anyone goes they take you with them. Say... I... were to go. Then I would take you with me.

Because I know you. I do.

I know you.

You have dreams. Dreams about flying, dreams about fall-ing, dreams that you don't understand. You have landscapes in your mind that you call your own. You try to be humble. You try to be honest. You know that it's better to keep your mouth shut and your eyes open, but it's very hard to do. You look for some small way to have some small way to have some small measure of immortality, but you're concerned that there will be nobody left to care. You hope that one day you'll under-stand something, but worry that maybe that's not the point. You wonder what's the big deal about sex anyway. And then suddenly, brilliantly remember. You go to movies, you think some of them are good and some of them are bad. You go to plays, even though you hate to be bored. Some nights you look up into the sky and remember what it felt like before every-thing felt so poisoned. And you think that love is a good thing.

See. I know you.

And so, say you die.

...And I know that's a scary thing but only because you don't know what happens, so I'm going to tell you.

When you die you float up to the ceiling and then you hit the ceiling and when you hit the ceiling you open your eyes and you find yourself in a white room in a kind of uncomfort-able chair. And every time you close your eyes your life plays itself out from the beginning, in real time. And so you decide to close your eyes and watch. And then when your life is over a woman comes into the room, she's your maternal grandmother when she was eighteen years old and you don't really recognize her because you didn't know her then. And she takes you by the arm and leads you out of the room, through a wheat field, across a beach, and over what looks like it might be the surface of the moon, to a room that is filled with photographs of every person whose eyes ever met yours. And then your grandma sits with you and goes through the pictures and she tells you a little bit about each person. And then you feel tired. So she leads you to an attic that is filled with mattresses from every bed you ever slept in. And in the centre of the room is the mattress from the bed in which you were conceived, and she tells you to lie down there, and you do, and you fall into a deep and restful sleep. And then you are woken up by the person you always felt you should have spent your life with but didn't. And then you get to spend a month together. And at the end of the month your dad comes to pick you up. And he drives you through every storm you ever slept through to a room with a table in it and three chairs. And he leaves you there standing before the table and three people enter the room: the first person you kissed, the first person you cursed, and the last person you saw dead. And they explain many many things to you, that you don't understand. And then they let you go through your best friend's closet and wear all your favourite stuff. And then they tell you that you must enter a room filled with people and you must tell these people something that they don't already know.

And before you can ask why you find yourself in a room full of people.

People you know. People you don't know. People you love. People you wished loved you. Strangers. Mostly strangers. And you try to tell these people something that they don't already know.

And then you realize that that is quite impossible. Because how can I tell you what you don't know when I don't even know what I know.

Note: In the above section it would be great if this audience, this evening, could be clearly included before the line "Strangers. Mostly strangers." For example if a phone had rung during the show HENRY would say, "People who forgot to turn off their cellphones." Or if someone had left to go to the washroom he would say, "People with small bladders." Or if someone had been sneezing, "People with colds." The actor must be alive and aware in the space on the evening. He must be Henry, or Henry must be him. Also, in the following section adjustments regarding Airport 75 *or the music played for Henry's dance or Elizabeth Taylor must be continued. And the Bay is a Canadian department store—not unlike Saks or Macy's or H&M.*

Well, I guess I know a few things.

My father had his moments.

My mother was a waitress, but she dressed like a nurse.

My sister was really my sister but I thought it would be more interesting if I said she was my mother.

And I can play the violin. It's just that some people don't call it a violin, some people call it a ukulele.

And I worked at the Bay for twenty-two years. In skin care. Gawd.

And my favourite song is "Finally" by CeCe Peniston.

And my favourite movie is *Airport 75* because Karen Black landed a plane in a skirt.

And my best day, if I had a best day, would be the day Elizabeth Taylor came to the Bay to sell her perfume and I got to hold her dog while Elizabeth Taylor went to bathroom.

And I don't have a problem being a homosexual I just have a problem with other people's problem with my not having a problem, maybe that's a problem I don't know.

And I never meant to be mean, I was just trying to be funny.

And I did write a book, it just hasn't been published. There's always hope.

And no I didn't set the fire, there was never any fire, I just wanted there to have been a fire because I wanted something to end.

And I think that love is a very good thing.

He waits for the end to happen.

And it still doesn't feel complete. It's like it's not over until the lights come up bright bright and then slowly slowly slowly fade to black and then Henry "Tom" Gallery, the Second, were to turn and walk away, singing a little song, and disappear forever.

But I can assure you, that is not going to happen.

He leaps out of his chair, tossing it aside.
Light: up bright, bright.
He regards the audience.
Light: slow slow slow fade as:

I am such a liar.

Slow slow slow fade to total black as HENRY turns and walks away, quietly singing a little song, and disappears forever.

End.

Daniel MacIvor is one of Canada's most-accomplished playwrights and performers. Winner of the prestigious Elinore
and Lou Siminovitch Prize, the GLAAD Award, the Governor
General's Literary Award, and many others, Daniel's plays
have been met with acclaim throughout North America.